D0439202

Table of Contents

ELEVATING YOUR GAME

Becoming a Triple-Impact Competitor

By Jim Thompson

Balance Sports Publishing, LLC, Portola Valley, California

Balance Sports Publishing, LLC
195 Lucero Way
Portola Valley, CA 94028
(650) 561-9586

PUBLISHER'S CATALOGING-IN-PUBLICATION DATA
Thompson, Jim, 1949-
    Elevating your game : becoming a triple-impact competitor / by Jim Thompson.
– 1st ed.

        p. ; cm.
        ISBN: 978-0-9821317-5-6

1. High school athletes–Psychology. 2. School sports–Psychological aspects. 3. School sports–Coaching. 4. Stress management for teenagers. I. Title.

GV706.4 .T56 2011
796/.042

FIRST EDITION
Printed in the United States of America

10 9 8 7 6   19 18 17 16 15

Designed by Elisa Tanaka

This one's for Rafi – a Triple-Impact Competitor from the beginning.

Special thanks to members of PCA's National Student-Athlete Advisory Board who gave invaluable input: Ryan Adachi, Molly Bagshaw, Kendall Baisden, Colleen Bush, Anne Canavati, Morgan Finegan, Natalie Gallo, Edgar Gutierrez, Rob Hart, Clare Herenda, Chase Hommeyer, Leslie Howard, Jaslyn Ivey, Sam Kelley, Callie King-Guffey, Katie Lanfranki, Frank Lima, Kelly Marren, Jessy Marshall, Megan Rauschnot, Kari Sandell, Ellyn Scally, Caraline Scally, Danny Swad, Zane Swanson, Trey Tickner, Ally Warson, Matt Wittlin, and Eve Zelinger. Thanks, too, to students and staff at Oak Ridge High School, and particularly to Carly Bettencourt, for valuable feedback and help along the way.

Additional thanks to the "brain trust" of high school coaches and advisors that helped inform and inspire this book: Doug Abrams, Nicholas Carlisle, Harry Colon, Tom Copeland, Anne Craighill, Jeaney Garcia, Alan Guffey, Lindsay Hampton, Ken Harkenrider, Molly Hellerman, Steve Henderson, Sandra Hietala, Curtis Higgins, Janet Holdsworth, Dann Jacobsen, Roch King, Cynthia King-Guffey, Laura Lauder, Ray Lokar, Rose Low, Dan McGee, Ruben Nieves, Andrew Oser, Dave Parsh, Kiha Pimental, Courtney Pollack, Rich Pruszynski, Jason Sacks, Craig Scott, David Shapiro, Tina Syer, Mike Terborg, Gabriel Thompson, and Kathy Toon.

Foreword
By Shane Battier

I'm excited about Jim Thompson's *Elevating Your Game* because the athletes I most admire, like Grant Hill, are Triple-Impact Competitors.

Grant took a moderately talented Duke basketball team to within one three-pointer of winning the national championship against Arkansas in 1994. No matter who was on the floor with Grant, you had a shot to win, and that's who I wanted to be – a guy who made the team better.

I had great coaches growing up, most of all, my dad. He taught me to help teammates be successful, because when you have success as a team, it's much sweeter than when you just have personal success. And I learned that when my team had success, I had personal success as well.

He taught me the importance of the next play. If you make an unbelievable move, you cross the guy over and make him fall, and dunk the basketball and get fouled and the crowd's going crazy, what do you do? Do you beat your chest and point to your girlfriend in the crowd and make a scene? No. You make the free throw, get back on defense, and try to do it again.

If you fall down and your guy scores and the crowd is laughing at you, do you sit there and pout? No. You pick yourself back up, dust off your shorts, and say, "That's not going to happen again. I'm going to stop him next time."

If you can live in the moment and go on to the next play, you're going to be successful no matter what you do in life.

Every coach and athlete is a steward of the game. I want every athlete to learn the game the way it's supposed to be played – not just wins and losses or X's and O's – but teamwork, work ethic, dedication, consistency.

I got involved with the Positive Coaching Alliance movement because I want every high school athlete to have the kind of experience I've had with sports. *Elevating Your Game* has great ideas and exercises to help you become a better player – but more important, a better person who will help make this society better. Our country needs Triple-Impact Competitors who make themselves, their teammates, and the game better, now more than ever. That's why *Elevating Your Game* is such an important book.

– Shane Battier
NBA star and former NCAA Player of the Year

Note: High school junior student-athletes may apply through May 31 for Triple-Impact Competitor® Scholarships. Visit **www.positivecoach.org/scholarships** for more information and to start your application, including an explanation on how you meet the Triple-Impact Competitor criteria of improving yourself, teammates and the game as a whole.

> Confidence, self-esteem, discipline, motivation. All these things I learned, whether I knew I was learning them or not, through sports.

Mia Hamm
Soccer Hall of Famer

Introduction
Three Ways to "Better"

In high school nothing was more important to me than being an athlete. It was part of my identity. If I performed well, I felt good about myself. If not, I didn't.

Two games frame my high school sports experience. Against Jamestown (North Dakota) High School in my senior year on the West Fargo High basketball team, I scored the tying basket with seconds left, then stole the ball and drove for the game winner.

Before our next game at Jamestown, my coach said their coach credited me with defeating them the last three times we had played: "That Thompson kid was the difference."

My final game against Jamestown was perhaps my worst game ever. I repeatedly turned the ball over, scored only a handful of points, and fouled out (unheard of for me).

It took me years to realize that the pressure I felt was responsible for my poor play. I felt I *had* to play well, that it was up to me, all by myself, to defeat Jamestown. Where before I just went out and played my game without worrying about how I did, this time I crashed and burned as I staggered under increased expectations. And I had no way to deal with increased pressure.

Since starting Positive Coaching Alliance in 1998, I've had the good fortune to work with some of the greatest coaches and athletes in the world. Some – like Phil Jackson, Summer Sanders, Doc Rivers, Dean Smith, and Julie Foudy – are household names. But many other outstanding coaches and athletes have also contributed their thinking and experience to the central questions of this book:

> ➤ **How do athletes elevate their game when it matters most?**
>
> ➤ **And why do so many athletes – like me against Jamestown – find their game going bad just when they need it the most?**

This book provides frameworks, ideas, and tools you can use to elevate your game. Consider the following three examples.

Louisiana State University pitcher Anthony Ranaudo had one of his worst outings of the season against Virginia on June 13, 2009. Instead of dwelling on his poor performance, Ranaudo said, "I just have to be able to flush it mentally and go out there with a new attitude and approach."

On June 23, in the finals of the NCAA College World Series, LSU lost to Texas 5-1 to force a third game in which the winner would become the NCAA Champion. The next day LSU defeated Texas 11-4. The winning pitcher? Anthony Ranaudo, who put aside his earlier failure to succeed in the biggest game of the year.

Kurt Warner had one of the greatest seasons any quarterback has ever had in 1999, culminating in a St. Louis Rams Super Bowl victory on January 30, 2000. A few years later, after injuries and inconsistency on the field, Warner lost his starting job to Marc Bulger. However, instead of pouting, Warner helped Bulger succeed, even though he knew it could keep him sidelined. Bulger did well that season and went on to become a two-time Pro Bowl selection.

Meanwhile, Warner was released by the Rams, picked up by the Giants, and ended up with the Arizona Cardinals, who chose him to mentor their young quarterback, Matt Leinart. Warner then led the Cardinals, a team given no chance to contend for a title, to the Super Bowl.

On April 26, 2008, Western Oregon University's Sara Tucholsky rounded first base after stroking the ball over the fence in the top of the second inning. In her excitement, she missed first base and, when she turned, injured a ligament in her right knee and crumpled to the ground in pain. Because her teammates had already scored, no one from her team could help her without her becoming an immediate out.

Central Washington University first baseman Mallory Holtman asked the umpire if she could help her. When he acknowledged that she could, she and teammate Liz Wallace gently carried Tucholsky around the bases so she could claim the home run she had earned.

These three stories illustrate athletes elevating their games.

> ➤ Anthony Ranaudo made himself better by focusing on the next game rather than sulking about the previous one, and won the NCAA Championship game.

> ➤ Kurt Warner gave his team a better chance to succeed when he made his teammate better, even though that teammate, Marc Bulger, took his starting job away. Because of the kind of teammate Warner was, he got another chance and made the most of it, leading his new team to the Super Bowl.

> ➤ Mallory Holtman made the game better with a remarkable display of Honoring the Game by helping her opponent, Sara Tucholsky, finish her home run, even though the two teams were fighting for an NCAA Division II playoff berth.

This book is about a mindset that can help you elevate your game like Ranaudo, Warner, and Holtman did. We call it the Triple-Impact Competitor, the gold standard for athletes.

■ The Hallmark of a Triple-Impact Competitor

If there is one word associated with a Triple-Impact Competitor, it is "better." A Triple-Impact Competitor is committed to better on three levels:

1) **Self:** Triple-Impact Competitors work hard to make themselves better by pursuing personal mastery.

2) **Teammates:** Triple-Impact Competitors are leaders who make those around them better.

3) **The Game:** Triple-Impact Competitors compete by a code of Honoring the Game which makes the game itself better.

Better is reflected in the Olympic Motto – "Citius, Altius, Fortius!" – "Faster, Higher, Stronger! "

Notice, in the premiere competition in the world – the Olympics – it isn't about being fast*est*, high*est*, strong*est*. If you are the best in the world in your event, you still want to get better. For the best, "better" is better than "best."

■ The Challenge

Being a Triple-Impact Competitor is not easy. The actions of Anthony Ranaudo, Kurt Warner, and Mallory Holtman required mental discipline and a commitment to maintain their values under pressure. But if you build a commitment to being a Triple-Impact Competitor into who you are as a person, you will find it can provide a larger meaning for your involvement in sports beyond who wins what game. And it will pay off for you in meaningful ways in the rest of your life.

Each chapter in this book focuses on a different aspect of being a Triple-Impact Competitor, offering fresh insights and tools gleaned from some of the world's best athletes, coaches, and sports psychology experts who are part of the Positive Coaching Alliance movement to transform the culture of high school and youth sports. Virtually all of us wish we had known about the insights and tools in this book when we were high school athletes.

We also include nine exercises so you can apply what you learn about becoming a Triple-Impact Competitor. Start with Exercise 1: Triple-Impact Competitor Self-Assessment on the following page to gauge the extent to which you make yourself, your teammates, and the game better. Then read on to discover how to truly elevate your game.

To what extent are you a Triple-Impact Competitor? Assess yourself on each of the statements below using a 1-5 scale (1 = never, 2 = seldom, 3 = sometimes, 4 = often, 5 = always).

Making Myself Better

_4_ 1. My coaches and teammates would say I give maximum effort in workouts, practices, and competitions.

_5_ 2. My coaches and teammates would say I have a teachable spirit. I accept feedback so I can learn and get better.

_3_ 3. I work hard on my mental game, using a variety of tools such as visualization, positive self-talk, and mistake rituals to allow me to move past failures quickly and refocus on the next play.

_2_ 4. I'm a "24-Hour Athlete" who manages diet, hydration, and sleep to optimize my performance on and off the field.

Making Teammates Better

_3_ 5. I'm on the lookout for leadership opportunities that help my team achieve its goals.

_5_ 6. My teammates would say I'm a positive teammate. I support my teammates by building them up. When I do criticize, I do it constructively and at the right time in the right way.

_4_ 7. My coaches and teammates would say I'm a team player who helps build strong team chemistry. My first priority is team success, and I adjust and accept my role to help my team.

Making the Game Better

_3_ 8. I honor the game by respecting the rules, opponents, officials, teammates, and myself.

_3_ 9. I use my status and influence as an athlete to improve my school community.

Everyone looks at the scoreboard. What's different with athletes with a mastery focus is that they have other ways of keeping the boat afloat when things don't tilt in their direction.

Joan Duda
Professor of Sport Psychology,
University of Birmingham (UK)

1.1 **The ELM Tree of Mastery**

SECTION

ONE

MAKING
YOUR
SELF
BETTER

What if I told you that you'll *win more* when you focus less on winning? It may seem counterintuitive, but it's true.

Triple-Impact Competitors make themselves better through a disciplined pursuit of mastery, a passionate quest to get better and better. Success on the field is a by-product of their focus on getting better, not winning. The scoreboard alone is a much too limited measure of mastery. So what if you beat the opposition but don't improve?

The easiest way to win is to compete against a weaker opponent. The University of Connecticut's women's basketball team, the powerhouse with the longest winning streak in college basketball history, would never lose a game if they only played elementary school teams. But it would prove nothing. The true test of a Triple-Impact Competitor is how you do compared to your best self, to what you could be.

This comes from having a worthy competitor, not one you can defeat easily without breaking a sweat. Great competitors want to test themselves against challenging opponents because they know that is the way to improvement, to mastery. A worthy opponent is a gift.

The path to mastery is illustrated by a concept called the **ELM Tree of Mastery**, which is based on more than 20 years of sport psychology research on how to reach one's potential. ELM stands for

---

E for Effort: Give your best every time. Leave it all out on the field.

L for Learning and improvement: No matter what happens on the scoreboard, focus on what you can take away to get better.

M for bouncing back from Mistakes: Setbacks and mistakes are inevitable on the road to Mastery. What's crucial is how you respond to them.

Research shows that the best route to top performance is to focus on what you can control and ignore what you can't.

➤ Bad weather? Can't control it, so don't focus on it.

➤ Not feeling great on the day of an important competition? Can't control how you feel, but you can control how you respond to your ailments.

➤ Bad call against you? Focus on getting yourself ready for the next play.

■ **Climbing the ELM Tree to the Scoreboard**

The ELM Tree is powerful because it leads to better results on the scoreboard. Athletes and teams that focus on mastery win more than those that make their primary goal trying to win.

Professor Joan Duda looked at athletes who competed in the 2000 Olympics and found that those who focused on mastery – getting better and doing the best they could – won more medals than comparable athletes focused on trying to win medals.*

---

* For more information about Professor Duda's research on sport motivation and optimal coaching environments, see http://www.sportex.bham.ac.uk/about/staff/joanduda.shtml

Focusing only on winning doesn't work. The one thing you can't control is what happens on the scoreboard. Winning and losing depend on the quality of your opponent's play, officials' calls, the way the ball bounces, and other things outside of your control.

If you focus on winning, which you can't control, you tend to get more anxious and less self-confident, both of which undercut how well you play.

On the other hand, you can control

> ➤ Your **E**ffort

> ➤ How much you **L**earn, and

> ➤ How you respond to **M**istakes.

Having this control reduces anxiety and increases self-confidence. Athletes who go into competitions with confidence and their anxiety under control tend to do well. That's the power of the ELM Tree, which we'll look at in greater depth in the next three chapters.

SECTION

ONE

MAKING
YOUR
SELF
BETTER   1.1 | Elevating Your Game | 10

It always bugs me when people call me a natural shooter. I spent many years in a gym working hard to become a "natural" shooter.

Chris Mullin
Member, NBA Hall of Fame

Effort as a Habit 1.2

N BA stars LeBron James and Carmelo Anthony learned something impor-tant as members of the US Olympic basketball team that won the 2008 Gold Medal in Beijing. They saw firsthand how hard their teammate Kobe Bryant worked *every day*, often starting at 6:30 a.m. to be the best basketball player he can be. Think about it. Kobe – rich, famous, arguably the best player in the world – gets up at dawn to practice. Many observers believe James and Anthony have both elevated their games, especially their defense – which is largely about effort – since being exposed to Bryant's work habits.

Along with cultivating a Teachable Spirit, which we'll discuss in the next chapter, there may be nothing more important to your ultimate success than fostering the habit of working hard. While most people think talent is the key to success, effort is more important. And, best of all, it's in your control because you control how hard you work.

Our culture gives us "either/or" messages. Either you've got it or you don't. You're smart or you're not. You're a good athlete or you're not. But it's not talent *or* effort. It's talent *and* effort. Talent and effort are intertwined.

But if you have to choose between them, effort is more important than talent because effort over time leads to skill and ability. And, as Chris Mullin discov-ered, if you work hard over a long time, people may even begin to call it talent.

On the other hand, talent without effort is just sad. The world is full of talented individuals who never learned to work hard and who, sooner or later, shuffle out of sight, never fulfilling their potential. Talent can be a trap that way.

■ Avoiding the Talent Trap

Carol Dweck, author of *Mindset: The New Psychology of Success,* identifies two common mindsets.

The first is the "fixed mindset," in which one sees one's ability as set. How hard you try doesn't matter much because you either have it or you don't. In fact, in this mindset you don't want to be seen as trying hard because that implies that you don't have it (talent).

This mindset is a dead-end because whether you succeed or not is determined by something totally outside your control — the amount of talent you are born with. If you believe your talent determines how successful you will be, you have fallen into the Talent Trap and you won't reach your potential.

The other mindset is the "Growth Mindset," in which you believe in your ability to grow and improve, regardless of where you start. With a Growth Mindset, your ultimate success is dependent on how hard you work, not on how much talent you were born with. And Dweck's research with college soccer players demonstrates this. She found that the more players believed their ability was a result of effort and practice (rather than talent), the more they improved over the course of a season.

Triple-Impact Competitors develop a Growth Mindset and talk to themselves in Growth Mindset language:

> ➤ "I can improve my serve if I **work hard at it.**"

> ➤ "I can learn to go strong to my left if I **work hard at it.**"

> ➤ "I can make 95 percent of my short putts if I **work hard on them.**"

SECTION

ONE

MAKING
YOUR
SELF
BETTER

They understand that setbacks are inevitable, and they respond to them with renewed effort. They may get discouraged from time to time because everyone does, but they understand that success comes from effort over time. Triple-Impact Competitors rise above their disappointment and figure out what they need to work on to do better next time.

▓ Effort Goals

Because they have a Growth Mindset, Triple-Impact Competitors set goals differently than most people. First of all, they write down their goals. Secondly, they use "Effort Goals" to help them get where they want to go.

Most people don't set goals at all, and those who do tend to set "outcome goals." Examples of outcome goals are averaging 20 points per game or making the all-star team. But outcome goals are often not within a person's control. You may perform at your best but not meet your outcome goals.

That's why Effort Goals are so powerful. Effort Goals are under your control because you can control how hard you work. And well-designed Effort Goals should, over time, move one toward Outcome Goals.

For example, a volleyball player may set an outcome goal of hitting at least four aces per match. A good Effort Goal might be to keep her head up and follow through on each serve.

Notice you can't control how many winning serves you hit, but you absolutely can control whether or not you keep your head up and follow through. And, if you do that every time, you'll hit more winners.

Most successful people set goals, and most unsuccessful people don't. Use Exercise 2 on the following page to help you set and achieve your goals.

Successful people set goals and work hard to achieve them. Unsuccessful people don't. The following framework, adapted from the research of Richard Lerner of Tufts University, is designed to help you accomplish your goals in sports and life.

Think of a GPS device, which contains your destination and step-by-step directions. The letters GPS represent steps in reaching your goals – Goal Selection, Plan of Action (the strategies you will pursue), and Shifting Gears (when things don't go as planned).

G – Goal Selection

Picking the right goals is crucial. Here are some guidelines for the G in your GPS.

- Pick challenging goals and visualize achieving them. For example, if you want to increase your vertical leap to be able to dunk a basketball, close your eyes and see and feel the excitement of elevating and dunking. If a goal doesn't energize you, you aren't likely to stick with it long enough to reach it. Recognize that a hard goal that you fail to achieve may cause you to improve more than achieving an easy goal.

- At the same time, avoid a "too-big" goal that may discourage you and cause you to give up on it. Set a time frame for interim goals that are achievable.

- Write your goals so you can see them. By writing them, you are signifying your commitment to achieve them.

- It's motivating to know your hard work will help others, so include goals to make teammates and the game better. Knowing your team needs you to improve your serve, for example, will help you follow through on practicing 50 extra serves every day.

- Make sure your goals work with each other. For example, avoid setting an athletic goal that takes so much time you won't be able to achieve your academic goals.

P – Plan of Action

Goals go nowhere without smart action, so energize the P in your GPS.

- What gets measured gets done. Divide goals into bite-size chunks and check progress with, for example, a chart you fill in each day.

- Set Effort Goals (see Chapter 1.2) in terms of time-on-task, such as, "I'll spend 5 hours this week working on stick handling."

- Make a "public commitment" to your effort goals. Commit to check in each week with a friend, parent, or coach.

- Visualize working on your goals in a specific place at a specific time. For example, tell yourself, "I'm going to sit down at my desk and study for 25 minutes as soon as I get home from practice."

- Reward progress. Tie something you enjoy to your Effort Goals. For example, I often reward myself for reaching my weekly writing goals by seeing a movie.

S – Shifting Gears

Most goals require adjustments along the way. Expect to shift gears at least once.

- Expect "inevitable setbacks." Rather than get discouraged when meeting a barrier, remember that setbacks are just part of life. Take them as a challenge.

- Remember to WAG: Watch, Ask, and Get coaching.

- Be willing to recalibrate your goals. That may mean changing an unrealistic goal without getting discouraged. Ask, "Do I need to work harder, try different strategies, or should I adjust my goal?"

The Most Important Thing

Don't worry about doing everything right in goal setting. The most important thing is to begin. Recalibrate goals and shift gears to new strategies if you run into problems. Use a chart like this one to help you commit to your goals and track your progress.

GOAL	PLAN	SHIFT
Lower my cross-country time 15 seconds by district meet.	● Add weekly interval training to up my speed.	● Developed shin splints at the end of week two.
	● Increase mileage by five miles each week.	● Cut back mileage for two weeks.
	● Get Lauren to run with me to make it more fun.	
	● Set up weekly check-in with coach.	

> I don't divide the world into the weak and the strong, or the successes and the failures, those who make it or those who don't. I divide the world into learners and non-learners.

Benjamin Barber
Author and scholar

Cultivating a Teachable Spirit 1.3

I n 1998, Washington State's Ryan Leaf and Tennessee's Peyton Manning were widely seen as the top two quarterbacks in the NFL draft. NFL fans were on fire with discussion about who would be the better pro.

At 6-foot-5 and 240 pounds, mobile with a strong, accurate arm, Leaf seemed like a can't-miss prospect. He also performed better in big games in college than Manning, which didn't hurt his draft prospects. Ultimately, Manning was drafted first by the Indianapolis Colts and Leaf second by the San Diego Chargers.

Many things affected Leaf's failure in his three turbulent seasons in the NFL, including a wrist injury on his throwing arm. But a key trait that separated Manning from Leaf was Manning's intense desire to get better. While Leaf fought with coaches and teammates and sometimes missed workouts and practices, Manning listened to coaches, watched film endlessly, embraced his teammates, and developed workout routines legendary for their toughness. Never satisfied with what he can do or with what he knows, Manning is coachable and determined to learn. As a result, Manning is a lock for the NFL Hall of Fame.

■ The Nobility of the Sponge

Having a Teachable Spirit is like being a sponge. Sponges seem lowly, but what makes them great is how they soak stuff up and grow in the process. Triple-Impact Competitors are sponge-like, hungry to learn, constantly on the lookout for ideas, tools, anything that will make them better.

If your coach yells at you for a mistake he never taught you about, as a Triple-Impact Competitor you shrug off the yelling and say to yourself, "This is unfair, but I'm not going to let my angry feelings keep me from improving." Most students in a class with a boring teacher tune out and do only enough to get by. With a Teachable Spirit, you ask, "This is boring, but what can I learn from it that will help me?"

Triple-Impact Competitors listen and learn and grow. But many athletes are not sponges. Think about teammates who thought they knew everything, who tuned out coaches and teammates alike, or simply weren't as committed as you. You may have a coach who didn't care what you or your teammates had to offer, even ideas that could have helped the team. Ultimately, an indifference to learning and new ideas limits a team's potential and reduces the fun of being on a team that works hard together.

What to do about it? Set an example and be a sponge. The world's greatest athletes, the world's greatest in any profession, are relentless learners.

■ The Freedom of the Fool

Often what keeps athletes from learning and growing is the fear of looking bad in public. George Leonard turns this idea on its head: "To be a learner, you've got to be willing to be a fool... How many times have you failed to try something new out of fear of being thought silly?"

Kelly Marren, a world class snowboarder and member of PCA's National Student-Athlete Advisory Board, described her experience: "When I first started snowboarding, it didn't bother me to look foolish trying to learn a trick. As I became more prominent, I realized that I was reluctant to try new tricks because I was afraid of being embarrassed." But Kelly remembered that the way to get better was to be willing to look foolish and deal with the discomfort that goes with it.

SECTION
ONE

MAKING
YOUR
SELF
BETTER

1.3 | Elevating Your Game | 18

Kelly has a robust Teachable Spirit and got past her fear, but imagine not try-ing something fun or interesting because you didn't want to look foolish. Yes, someone might mock you if you look foolish, but the really foolish person is the one who doesn't learn. When you think about it, there is great freedom in being willing to play the fool.

■ The WAG Approach

Here are three effective, simple ways to learn in sports: **W**atch, **A**sk, and **G**et coaching, which I refer to as "WAG."

If a teammate knows how to do something you don't, *watch* what she does and see if you can replicate it. Some athletes deal well with pressure. How do they do it? Watch them. Some athletes are really good at preparing themselves for a competition. What do they do to prepare? Your team's leaders command re-spect from their teammates and inspire confidence in ways that makes the team better. What, if anything, do they do that you can copy?

If watching doesn't get you there, ask your teammates and coaches. Many great competitors even ask opponents how they do things. Some of the top pro and college coaches in various sports get together after the season to share ideas and try to anticipate the next big trends in their sport. Even though they com-pete with each other during the season, they cooperate to learn together and increase all of their capabilities in the off-season.

But some things can't be acquired simply from watching and asking. Mastering them requires that you get coaching. A coach can see things you don't. Bill Sweet-enham, the former Australian Olympic swim team coach, once explained why ath-letes need coaches: "The athlete feels the water, the coach sees the stroke."

Some things we just can't learn on our own, at least in a reasonable time period. We need a coach who can "see our stroke" and help us get to new levels of per-formance. A Triple-Impact Competitor with a robust Teachable Spirit seeks out coaching.

It may seem odd to ask your coach to help you. After all, isn't that his job? Yes, but coaches have so much going on they can overlook opportunities to help players improve. By asking for specific coaching, you are signaling to your coach that you are primed to learn.

Be persistent. Your coach may agree to help you but fail to do so. If so, make it easier for him by being more specific: "I really want to learn that skill. Is there a day this week you can work with me on this after practice?"

■ Fueling Performance

In recent years, many elite athletes have shown their teachable spirit by embracing emerging knowledge from the field of sports nutrition to modify their diet as a way of getting better. Test your knowledge by taking the Sport Nutrition Quiz featured in Exercise 3 on the following page. Then apply what you learn so you can fuel even better performance.

SECTION

ONE

MAKING
YOUR
SELF
BETTER   1.3 | Elevating Your Game | 20

The best athletes recognize that there is a strong connection between their nutrition and how they perform. What do you know about how to "eat to compete?" Take the quiz below. Then read about the answers on the following pages. In the process, you should improve your nutrition I.Q. and, by doing so, give yourself an edge on the competition.

Mark each statement true or false.

_____ 1. Some foods are like health magic; others are evil and have no nutritional value.

_____ 2. Don't snack. It is bad for you.

_____ 3. Water can make the difference between winning and losing.

_____ 4. If you want to build muscle, load up on protein – the more, the better.

_____ 5. Breakfast is the most important meal of the day.

_____ 6. It is possible to use food to help your muscles recover between practices and competitions.

_____ 7. The best meal to eat right before exercise should be easily digestible and not heavy on fat or calories.

_____ 8. Stick to a diet with a few healthy foods that you eat over and over.

Sports Nutrition Quiz Answers

1. Some foods are like health magic; others are evil and have no nutritional value.

False. Every food carries some nutrient your body can use. But some foods carry nutrients way better than others. Sports nutritionist Chris Carmichael categorizes foods into three categories: quality carriers, empty carriers, and pollutant carriers.

- Quality carriers like whole-grain cereal or bread, salmon, chicken breasts, brown rice, and spinach are like yachts. They carry nutrients in style.

- Empty carriers like iceberg lettuce, pretzels, and white rice are like riding in a rowboat.

- Pollutant carriers are foods like doughnuts, fatty chips or candy bars, many fast foods, French fries, fried chicken, and heavily processed foods. Nutrients in them are on a garbage barge. Taking in lots of garbage – saturated fat, sugar, and chemicals – with your nutrients will bog you down and hurt your athletic performance, not to mention your long-term health.

2. Don't snack. It is bad for you.

False. Athletes burn plenty of calories and, as a result, get hungry. Fuel up on healthy snacks between meals. Fruit, bagels, nuts, yogurt, a health bar, and juice can elevate your game. For many athletes, consuming a snack of 200 to 300 calories within an hour or two of a performance can improve results. And, for some sports like baseball or tennis or for lengthy workouts that can last for hours, a snack during the activity helps athletes maintain energy and mental clarity.

3. Water can make the difference between winning and losing.

True. Hydrated athletes compete better than dehydrated ones. Your body is comprised of 60 percent water, and 62 percent of that is contained in muscles and blood tissue. When you don't drink adequate fluids, your body temperature rises and the blood volume in your muscles decreases. Smaller muscles equal less strength. Drink lots of liquid — water or sports drinks — throughout the day and during hard workouts and competitions.

4. If you want to build muscle, load up on protein — the more, the better.

False. We used to think that eating raw eggs, protein shakes, steaks, and tuna fueled big gains in muscle mass and improved athletic performance. Now we know that loading up on protein doesn't do much because your body isn't equipped to process extra protein. Elite athletes may need a little more protein, but not much more. And most of the protein in protein shakes is flushed down the toilet. Your body just can't absorb it.

5. Breakfast is the most important meal of the day.

Probably. In the morning, your body has just experienced a 10- to 14-hour fast. Your glycogen stores — what gives you the energy to operate well in school and in sports — are low and need to be replenished. Little time for breakfast? Think simple. A bowl of cereal, a yogurt, boiled eggs, a muffin, a health bar, or toast with peanut butter all make good starts to a day and will help you be your best.

6. It is possible to use food to help your muscles recover between practices and competitions.

True. This is critical to maintaining energy and motivation during a long, hard season. If you don't fuel up properly between practices and competitions, your body will wear down and you can hit a wall. What to do?

● Eat something for breakfast.

● Don't skip lunch if you can help it.

- Eat snacks as needed and consume a pre-practice snack that doesn't upset your stomach.

- Keep yourself hydrated.

- After workouts, eat a recovery meal that contains carbohydrates, fat, and protein. In the hour after intense exercise your body will soak up the nutrients from a peanut butter and jelly or turkey sandwich, an energy bar, or a smoothie. This aids recovery and gives you more energy the next day.

7. The best meal to eat right before exercise should be easily digestible and not heavy on fat or calories.

True. This question is way too easy, right? But how many athletes do you know who eat greasy fast foods right before a practice or game? Fatty foods take longer to digest. That's why they can just sit in your stomach. And that's why they can make you sick or slow you down at just the wrong time – when you want to be at your best for yourself and for your teammates.

8. Stick to a diet with a few healthy foods that you eat over and over.

False. Actually, a variety of grains, meat, vegetables, dairy, nuts, and other foods is what you want to shoot for. Sports nutritionist Nancy Clark tells athletes to eat 35 different foods each week. But getting this can be hard, especially when you are busy or don't even do the shopping. Do the best you can and if you feel overwhelmed, consider Michael Pollan's advice in *Food Rules,* "Eat food. Not too much. Mostly plants."

Note: These pages contain a few general nutritional guidelines for athletes. Talk with your coach about specific nutritional advice for your sport.

Sources: Nancy Clark's *Sport's Nutrition Guidebook* and Chris Carmichael's *Food for Fitness.*

Great players have the ability to flush mistakes. That ability is like learning a new language. "This simply was a mistake. Let us learn from it and move on." This is easier said than done.

Sue Enquist
UCLA Softball Coach (ret.)

Embracing Mistakes to Become Your Best 1.4

You can never be your best if you fear mistakes. If you are afraid of making mistakes, you will play tentatively, and tentative players usually get beat.

Being afraid of making a mistake is worse than making one. Let me say that another way. It is better to *make* a mistake than to be *afraid* of making one.

Sports are filled with mistakes. The best baseball hitters fail about 70 percent of the time. Great shooters in basketball miss roughly half their shots. Elite cornerbacks in football and closers in baseball cultivate "short memories" to quickly put mistakes behind them and prepare for what's next. Every athlete makes mistakes – lots of them.

What separates great athletes from the rest is how they deal with mistakes. Strange as it sounds, to become a Triple-Impact Competitor, you must embrace – not fear – mistakes.

▓ Becoming a Player Who Makes Things Happen

Legendary UCLA basketball coach John Wooden, who led his teams to 10 NCAA championships, said, "The team that makes the most mistakes will probably win. . . The doer makes mistakes, and I wanted doers on my team – players who make things happen."

Consider this statement by Wayne Gretzky, widely regarded as the greatest hockey player of all time: "You miss 100 percent of the shots you never take."

Despite the fact that Gretzky was not particularly big or strong or fast, he was a great competitor who focused on what he wanted to accomplish rather than worry about mistakes he might make. He was a player who made things happen.

With this attitude toward mistakes, Wooden's players and Gretzky were able to play more aggressively. In almost every sports situation, the more aggressive athlete or team usually does better than the more timid athlete or team. But fear of making a mistake is deadly for aggressiveness and leads to timid play.

How do you become a player who makes things happen? By developing a fearlessness about mistakes that comes from knowing you can quickly rebound from them. And that comes from having a mistake ritual that you can count on.

■ Using a Mistake Ritual to Develop Mental Toughness

A mistake ritual is something you do and say to transform your fear of mistakes so you don't play timidly. It helps you quickly reset so you can focus on the next play rather than beating yourself up for making a mistake.

A popular and effective mistake ritual is "The Flush." You react to a mistake with a motion like flushing a toilet while saying, "Flush it. Next play!"

Then you force your attention on the next play. Even though your inner voice may want to chastise you for making a mistake, refuse to allow the negativity to stay in your mind. If necessary, repeat, "Flush it! Next play!" and make the flushing motion again.

Over time, using a mistake ritual in this way builds mental toughness. The key is to focus on what you want to do the next play, knowing you can recover quickly if you do make a mistake. The more you do this, the more your mental toughness grows.

SECTION
ONE

MAKING
YOUR
SELF
BETTER

If "The Flush" doesn't feel right to you, try one of these other options or make a mistake ritual of your own. Which one you use isn't important, but using one is.

> ➤ "No Sweat:" Wipe your fingers across your forehead as if flicking sweat from your brow. "No sweat. Forget it. Next play!"

> ➤ "Brush It Off:" Motion as if brushing dirt off your shoulder. "Brush it off. Next play."

■ Always the Most Important Play

Many people enjoy debriefing a game and deciding which play was the most important. But the most important play is always the same for a Triple-Impact Competitor: the next play.

In sports there is almost always a next play. The athlete who beats herself up over the last play is not going to be ready for it. One coach uses the acronym NBA to help his players rebound from mistakes. NBA stands for Next Best Action. Instead of focusing on a mistake, players focus on what they most need to do next.

Here is Stanford women's volleyball coach John Dunning, whose teams have won three NCAA titles, on the next play:

> "So many kids think they're great competitors because they growl the loudest or cuss the loudest. I define a competitor as the person who is most often ready to play and win the next play. You've got to get the last play out of your mind, except the part that educates you. The person who consistently is most ready to win the next play is the person I want on my side of the net – not the growler."

■ What Are Mistakes Good For?

Let's stay with Coach Dunning a bit longer: get rid of the last play "except the part that educates you." Triple-Impact Competitors use mistakes to get better, by quick in-game adjustments or by setting them aside for the next practice.

Great athletes look at mistakes or failure as feedback. The trick is to know what to do with that feedback. Mistakes in a competition can lead to immediate adjustments, like when you've guessed wrong about your opponent's strengths or weaknesses. Or, you may have forgotten your role on a given play or lost your focus at a critical moment, so you increase your concentration and refocus on your role.

But some mistakes need to be "parked" and returned to later. If you are a swimmer and mistiming your flip turns in an important meet, concentrate on making better flip turns. At the same time, make a mental note to work on your turns in the next practice. That's "parking" a mistake. There is no time to break down your mechanics during the competition. That's all right. Relax, flush the mistake, focus on the next play, and work on it later.

■ A Championship Turn-Around

Having the right mindset about mistakes can make a huge difference on the scoreboard. Midway through the 2004 season, with the Cal State Fullerton Titans baseball team's record at 15-16, the coach brought in sports psychology consultant Ken Ravizza to work with the team.

Ken installed a coin bank in the form of a toilet in the dugout (the handle made the sound of a toilet flushing). Players began flushing their bad plays down the toilet when they came in from the field. Ravizza also asked them to imagine they had a miniature toilet on their belts so they could flush bad plays before they got into the dugout.

The result was dramatic and immediate. The Titans were able to leave their bad plays behind, focus on the "next play," and perform to their capabilities. After implementing the mistake ritual, the Titans went 32-5. They qualified for the NCAA College World Series and promptly lost their first game in the double-elimination tournament. They won their way back up through the loser's bracket to play Texas in the championship game, needing to beat the Longhorns twice in a row, which they did. Cal State Fullerton used the power of a mistake ritual to help become national champions.

SECTION

ONE

MAKING
YOUR
SELF
BETTER

A mistake ritual doesn't make a champion out of a mediocre team. But it allows teams to play up to their potential, which for the Titans was national championship caliber. Use Exercise 4 on the following page to develop your own mistake ritual.

Triple-Impact Competitors adopt a different mindset about mistakes. They recognize that mistakes are inevitable. As a result, they don't fear them. To help recover from mistakes, Triple-Impact Competitors use mistake rituals to allow them to quickly refocus on the most important play – the next one. Over time, they develop a mental toughness to bounce back from mistakes, which also gives them the confidence to compete aggressively on every play.

1. In the space below, describe the mistake ritual you plan to use this season. It may be one of the three mentioned in Chapter 1.4 (The Flush, No Sweat, or Brush It Off), or one that you create on your own.

2. Then identify at least one teammate or coach with whom you will share your new mindset about mistakes so they can support your effort throughout the season to recover quickly from mistakes. You can describe your mistake ritual to them so they can reinforce it from the field or sideline after you've made a mistake.

My Mistake Ritual ___is to not think___

___about it until after the game___

___

___

___

I will share my new approach toward mistakes with

___Anitra___

> # It's not the will to win that matters—everyone has that. It's the will to prepare to win that matters.

Paul "Bear" Bryant
Hall of Fame college football coach

Getting a Mental Edge: Preparing to Compete 1.5

When I speak to high school athletes around the country, I often ask if they have a mental game. Some hands go up, but the looks on many faces tell me that they are not sure what that means.

Athletes without mental games do well if things go well. If not, they can't adjust to adversity and fail to perform to their ability. But some athletes develop a mental game they can rely on when things go bad so they are not at the mercy of events. They can give their best effort even when everything seems to be going wrong.

Think about the statement at the top of this chapter. Everyone wants to win, but just wanting to win doesn't do it. Preparation is the key. Most high school athletes prepare physically, but few prepare as hard mentally.

This chapter will help you prepare for competition in ways you may have never considered. Sport psychology teaches that mental preparation is as important as physical training and game-time execution. Here are tools to help you develop your mental game.

■ Becoming an Intentional Visualizer

Visualization has become a staple of great performers in all realms, but especially sports. It may seem mysterious, but we do it all the time. Visualization is so much a part of our lives that we often don't even recognize it as such.

For example, if someone asks you how to get to your school, you mentally rehearse how you would make the trip yourself. "Go down two blocks and make a left at Colfax Road. Then you go three blocks..." That is visualization.

The key is to become an *intentional* visualizer and use visualization to improve your performance. I recommend you add two kinds of visualization to your mental game tool kit: "mental rehearsal" and "catastrophization."

■ Mental Rehearsal

Here's Hall-of-Fame pitcher Nolan Ryan (quoted in *Mind Gym* by Gary Mack):

> "The night before a game I lie down, close my eyes, relax my body, and prepare myself for the game. I go through the entire lineup of the other team, one batter at a time. I visualize exactly how I am going to pitch to each hitter and I see and feel myself throwing exactly the pitches that I want to throw. Before I ever begin to warm up at the ballpark, I've faced all of the opposition's hitters four times and I've gotten my body ready for exactly what it is I want to do."

One kind of visualization is simply rehearsing what "I want to do." Notice that Ryan saw and felt himself doing what he wanted to do. The more senses you bring into play when you visualize, the better.

Begin by visualizing yourself successfully completing a skill such as making a catch, a putt, or a serve. Find a quiet place to sit and picture yourself completing the skill with perfect form. It's crucial that you see yourself doing it exactly right because practice doesn't make perfect, but perfect practice does.

Visualize yourself in the zone – making the big plays, making your teammates better, handling whatever happens with

SECTION

ONE

MAKING
YOUR
SELF
BETTER

1.5 | Elevating Your Game | 32

calmness and class. Start small. Nolan Ryan probably didn't start out by visualizing an entire game. Start with the beginning of the competition and see yourself doing what you want to do. Then pick out some challenging situations and see yourself successfully doing what you want.

In addition to the testimony of elite athletes like Ryan who say visualizing made them better, research shows that visualizing can improve a skill. One study showed that players who practiced shooting for 30 minutes and visualizing free throws for 30 minutes each day improved significantly more than players who practiced their shot for 60 minutes each day. Visualization with practice improved performance more than the same amount of time of practice alone. So give it a try.

■ Catastrophization

When Nancy Ditz set her sights on winning the Los Angeles Marathon in 1987, the heat concerned her. She feared not having a water bottle available when she needed it late in the race. She visualized remaining calm, not wasting energy on things she couldn't control. At one point during the race, her water bottle wasn't where it should have been, but she remained calm, just as she had visualized. She went on to win the L.A. Marathon because she had prepared for the worst with a tool I call "catastrophization."

A catastrophe is something that goes terribly wrong. With catastrophization, you visualize things happening exactly as you hope they will *not* happen. And then – *and this is crucial* – you visualize yourself continuing on with your best effort and prevailing.

You imagine everything going wrong at the beginning of a competition. You double fault your serves. You score an own-goal. You dribble the ball off your foot and miss an easy lay-up. You walk the bases loaded in the first inning.

You see yourself remain calm, confident you can do the only thing you have to do right now – make the next play. See yourself serve an ace, assist a teammate who heads the ball into the goal, hustle back to prevent an easy basket, get the next hitter to ground the ball back to you for a 1-2-3 double-play, after which you get the third out on a pop-up.

It is comforting to feel in your bones that you can prevail in a worst-case situation. Catastrophization helps you develop your mental game so you never let the emotional discomfort of being in a tough spot keep you from persevering.

■ Internal and External Cameras

You can visualize as you see out your own eyes with what I call the "internal camera," which is good for rehearsing a skill. Feel yourself serving, see your serve hit just as it does when you actually hit the ball.

Also visualize with the "external camera," as if you were watching yourself on videotape to show what you look like when you are doing it right. Experiment with both cameras because both will help you develop your "visualization muscle." The external camera helps you develop a mental blueprint of the proper motion you want to do, while the internal camera gives a taste of what your actual experience in the moment will be.

■ Preparing for "Off Days"

Most athletes have a Plan A, the way they like to compete that plays to their strengths. Former Boston Celtics great Larry Bird was a fantastic outside shooter and liked to shoot the three-pointer to set up his drives to the basket. But some days his outside shot wasn't dropping. Rather than get discouraged, Bird kept himself in the game with Plan B – work to get inside position for offensive rebounds. His Plan C was to move to open spaces to free up his teammates, set picks, and do whatever else was needed to help his team.

Bird's advance planning got him into the Basketball Hall of Fame. Here's a plan that Jessy Marshall, a member of PCA's National Student-Athlete Advisory Board, developed before several summer basketball tournaments.

SECTION
ONE

MAKING
YOUR
SELF
BETTER

1.5 | Elevating Your Game | 34

➤ Plan A: Drive to the bucket and either make the basket or get fouled.

➤ Plan B: Look for the pull-up shot off a screen or off the catch.

➤ Plan C: Drive and kick to a teammate that is open.

Jessy: "I know I'll execute each of the plans at one time or another in the game. I mentally go over all three plans repeatedly, so I can take what the defense gives me and make it work to my advantage."

You'll improve your performance on off days if you have back-up plans. Knowing ahead of time what you will do if Plan A isn't working can help you quickly transition to Plan B. A great Plan B is to focus on effort. If your offense isn't clicking, focus on working harder on defense. In many sports offensive attacks are started by tough defense.

Whatever your sport, you can hone your mental game by identifying your Plan A and preparing plans for what to do when it isn't working.

> # Where does the power come from to see the race through to its end? From within.
>
> **Eric Liddell**
> **Scottish Olympic Gold Medalist**

1.6 Getting a Mental Edge: During the Game

By the end of the third quarter in Game 3 of the 2010 NBA Finals, the Los Angeles Lakers' 17-point lead had shrunk to six, and the Boston Celtics had momentum going into the fourth quarter. Realizing his Lakers' teammates were demoralized, Derek Fisher asked if someone had told them before the game that they would start the fourth quarter ahead by six, would they have been happy about it? They all agreed they would have loved going into the last quarter with a six-point lead, which is, after all, where they were. Fisher's "reframing" question elevated their spirits, and the Lakers went on to win by seven points.

Mental preparation is crucial to high performance. But preparation gets you only so far because even the best plan can't anticipate everything that will happen in a competition. Sometimes you have to rise to the occasion in the moment. Here are some tools to help you deal with the various pressures that inevitably arise in the heat of competition.

■ Reframing to Increase Resilience

Once in the middle of a hard 10-mile run, I encountered a long muddy patch, and my shoes became caked with mud. My frustration grew with every step as I realized how tired I was and how far I still had to run.

SECTION
ONE
———
MAKING
YOUR
SELF
BETTER

But I thought of the special plyometric shoes my son, Gabriel, wore to improve his foot speed and vertical leap. What was so different about my running with a few extra pounds of mud on my soles? Thinking of my muddy shoes as intensifying my workout transformed my negative emotions, and I was able to enjoy the extra effort needed to finish my run.

Like Derek Fisher, I "reframed" my situation, something that photographers and filmmakers do to get a story right and get the right story. A certain take on a scene may not be right, so the filmmaker looks at the situation from different angles until she finds the one that tells the story she wants to tell.

Reframing is a three-step process:

1) Something disrupts your plans.

2) You experience negative emotions, like disappointment, discouragement, or sadness.

3) Rather than allowing that initial reaction to stick, you reframe and ask how you can make something good come from it.

You don't deny that it happened. You don't pretend it's not as bad as it is. You confront the reality and reframe the event so that it tells a story that will help you transform your negative emotions into positive ones.

Chris McLachlin, the legendary basketball and volleyball coach at Honolulu's Punahou School, tells of a coach of a volleyball team with a record good enough to be the top seed in a big tournament. But instead of a first game at home against the weakest opponent, they ended up traveling to play a strong team. He was upset, but his players, who had learned to reframe, took the better mental approach.

"Coach, traveling isn't so bad. We can play music on the bus. We can do our homework. It will be fun." Another player: "We want to win this tournament, so isn't it better if we play a tougher team in the first round so we'll be sharper in the later rounds when we play the top teams?" With these players' ability to reframe, it's not surprising that they did go on to win the tournament.

Used regularly, reframing can become a habit — a powerful tool to increase resilience. Knowing you can reframe and rebound from setbacks increases your poise. And resilience and poise contribute to success.

■ Control Your Emotions with a Self-Control Routine

Players who let their emotions control them can't play their best. That doesn't mean you have to be an emotionless robot. Competition brings out some of our strongest emotions: fear, anger, frustration, elation. That's natural. A key to elevating your game is developing an ability to channel those emotions productively. You need to control your emotions rather than allowing them to control you.

How do you handle your emotions when you are getting beat by a lesser opponent, being yelled at by your coach, feeling the sting of a cheap shot, or dealing with a bad call? That's key. Because if you retaliate, lose focus on the next play, sulk, or lash out at teammates or officials, you'll hurt your performance and that of others around you.

So, what can you do? Develop a self-control routine. It might involve deep breaths, self-talk ("Let it go!"), or tapping your helmet. You might walk to a different location and separate yourself from the action momentarily. A tennis player may go to the back fence and refocus. A pitcher might leave the mound momentarily. In sports where breaks don't happen, you'll need to refocus more quickly and do it in your mind only. That's okay. You be in charge. Don't let negative and destructive emotions run the show.

■ Transformational Self-Talk   .

Self-talk is a big idea in sport psychology because "we are what we eat" mentally as well as physically. If you feed yourself a lot of negative statements about yourself, it harms both your sense of possibility and your performance.

Everyone engages in self-talk. And even though most of the time most people aren't aware of it, it has a big impact on us. Most of the self-talk people engage in is negative. "I better not strike out." "This just isn't my day." "What will my friends say

SECTION
ONE
————
MAKING
YOUR
SELF
BETTER

if I lose?" So often we focus on the negative. And when we make a mistake, we tend to come down hard on ourselves and make blistering statements about how bad we are.

Imagine trying to play your best if your mind is filled with negative garbage. A player on the receiving end of negative self-talk is not a pretty sight. So Triple-Impact Competitors work hard to transform their negative self-talk.

Here's a three-step process called "Transformational Self-Talk" to counteract negative self-talk and get back on the right track.

1) **Make your self-talk a true statement by expressing it as a** *feeling.* When I screw up, I often say to myself, "You are an idiot!" Am I an idiot? Maybe, maybe not. But what is absolutely true is that I **feel** like an idiot. To make my self-talk absolutely true, I change it to, **"I** *feel* **like an idiot."**

2) **Use the Power of a Big BUT.** The word "but" is powerful. When we use it, we degrade or devalue whatever comes before. We all know when someone says "but" it means something negative is coming to devalue what was just said. So add "but" to your feeling statement to degrade it. **I feel like an idiot,** *but…*

3) **End with "I'm-the-kind-of-person-who."** Think about the kind of competi-tor you want to be, and tell yourself what will help you in this moment. Re-member, you are what you eat, so end your statement with something that reinforces your ability to keep going. **"I** *feel* **like an idiot,** *BUT* **I'm the kind of person** *who refuses to give up!"*

You have now transformed your negative self-talk into something that can keep you going in the face of adversity.

■ Prevent Choking with the 3 B's

Athletes at all levels worry that they will "choke" in the clutch. Let me be clear about what choking is and isn't. Choking is *not* failing to make a play. Choking is *not* getting beat on a great play by your opponent. Those things happen all the time and, while unfortunate, they are not the result of choking.

Choking is failing to perform an action in a high-pressure game situation that we can routinely perform in practice or games when the stakes are low. If I routinely make 9 of 10 free throws in practice, but miss several in a row at the end of a close play-off game, it may well be that I am choking.

Few athletes want to talk about choking. There is an unspoken belief that if you talk about choking, you may then be more likely to choke. But facing that fear allows you to develop an antidote to choking, like the 3 B's: Breathe, Bounce, & Break.

➤ **Breathe:** When we are afraid of choking, we literally don't get enough air into our system. Without proper breathing, we are unlikely to make the play. So the first B is Breathe. Take a couple of deep breaths, and feel the oxygen getting into your system.

➤ **Bounce:** We also tend to lose feeling of the ground in our feet when we get really nervous. So Bounce up and down a few times like a boxer warming up for a match, and get re-rooted to the earth.

➤ **Break:** As a high school football player, I was always nervous until I made contact with an opponent. Once I hit someone or someone hit me, the nervousness disappeared. So, the third B is Break. Clap your hands together briskly to simulate contact with the opposition.

The 3 B's make it much more likely you will be able to execute the play the way you are able to in practice.

Hone Your Mental Edge

You now have a set of tools that sports psychologists routinely use with elite athletes. Use Exercise 5 on the following page to create a plan to improve your mental game. While these tools don't guarantee success, they give you a greater chance to do your best — and a distinct mental edge over most other high school athletes.

SECTION

ONE

MAKING
YOUR
SELF
BETTER

Place check marks next to the mental game tools from Chapters 1.5 and 1.6 that you want to use right away. Then make a plan to use them.

Preparing to Compete

____ **Visualization: Rehearsal:** Visualize yourself in the "zone," performing at your best, doing things all the right ways.

____ **Visualization: Catastrophization:** Visualize "worst-case scenarios," and then visualize yourself continuing to work hard and prevailing.

____ **Preparing for "Off Days:"** Have alternative plans when your "A-game" does not come easily to you.

During the Game

____ **Reframing:** Re-cast what seem like problematic situations into favorable opportunities.

____ **Self-Control Routine:** Develop routines to make sure you don't let your emotions derail you.

____ **Transformational Self-Talk:** Transform negative self-talk to make it positive.

____ **Prevent Choking with the 3 B's:** Overcome the fear and nervousness that can accompany pressure situations using Breathe, Bounce, and Break.

Mental Game Action Plan

How will you begin to integrate these tools into your mental game?

_____

_____

_____

When you know it's a game, you've already won.

Andrew Oser
Author of *How Alternation*
Can Change Your Life

1.7 Non-Attachment: Separating Identity from Performance

Entering the 1992 U.S. Olympic trials, Dan O'Brien was riding high, having recently set the world record in the grueling, 10-event decathlon whose winner is usually considered the world's greatest athlete. In the pole vault, O'Brien took his first jump at 15 feet-9 inches, after passing on four lower opening heights.

O'Brien had easily cleared 16-1 in warm-ups and routinely cleared 15-9 in practice, but he hit the crossbar in his first two attempts. On his final attempt, he didn't even reach the bar. Zero points in the vault meant O'Brien missed the U.S. Olympic Team, so the top decathlete in the world sat out the 1992 Barcelona Olympics.

Sometimes we want something so badly our desire gets in the way. We get "attached" when something seems so important we can't feel good about ourselves unless we achieve it. Our self-worth is threatened, our efforts become feverish and ineffective, and we may even panic.

We've all had teammates so anxious about a last-second play they aren't able to take their best shot. This happens at all levels of sports. After the Los Angeles Lakers edged the Boston Celtics in the 2010 NBA Finals, Kobe Bryant said of his poor

SECTION
ONE
———
MAKING
YOUR
SELF
BETTER

shooting early in Game 7, "You know, I just wanted it so bad... And the more I tried to push, the more it kept getting away from me."

In pressure moments, competitors can be helped by a concept called "non-attachment." Non-attachment is the ability to detach oneself from the *outcome* of a performance. Top performing athletes understand that the result of an athletic contest does not define them as a person. When athletes define themselves by results, the desire to succeed can produce a hyped-up emotional state that robs them of their best effort.

■ Panning Back to See the Big Picture

One way to achieve non-attachment is "panning back," a technique filmmakers use to enhance a story. In a tight shot, we see a person surrounded by bad guys about to attack. As the camera pans back to show a larger area, we see the hero entering the scene to save the day.

Panning back helps us see our bigger picture, for example, that our life will not be ruined if we fail in a competition. When I pan back, I hold an imaginary camera up to my eye with one hand and rotate the other backwards as if turning the crank on an old movie camera.

This physical motion helps me look for the bigger picture: "If I fail here, can I survive and thrive?" The answer is almost always yes, which helps me detach from the results, so my efforts are more effective.

■ We Don't Always Know What's Best for Us

Cultivating non-attachment makes sense because we often don't know what is best for us, as in this story adapted from *Thinking Body, Dancing Mind* by Chungliang Al Huang and Jerry Lynch.

A farmer's son was distraught when he left the gate open and the family's only horse escaped. "This is the worst thing that could happen," he told his father, who replied, "How do you know that?" The next day, their horse returned leading a herd of wild horses. The son said, "This is the best thing that could happen." Father: "How do you know that?"

When the son broke his arm trying to tame one of the wild horses, he said, "This is the worst thing that could happen." Father again: "How do you know that?" Shortly thereafter, military recruiters came to enlist all the young men in the area. They didn't take the injured son, who exulted, "This is the best thing that could happen." I think you know what his father said.

Sometimes what seems like a bad thing turns out to be a good thing. We should be slow to conclude that we know the ultimate impact of what happens to us.

■ Separating Your Identity From Your Performance

Winning a game or acing a test doesn't determine your value as a human being. It may seem that way, but it's not true.

When you begin to believe your identity is not dependent on your performance, you begin to free yourself from the pressure to succeed. That leads to self-confidence and a lightness of being that make it more likely that you will succeed.

As the view from a mountain top is different than from the plains below, non-attachment can provide you with a higher, better perspective on your life. When we are non-attached we can work hard and smart to achieve our goals without feeling like we *have* to achieve them to show we are worthwhile.

Those who achieve great things usually have the ability to pan back to see the bigger picture, to become detached from the need to win, which helps them rise above momentary setbacks. And, by the way, this is exactly what Dan O'Brien did when he won the 1996 Olympic gold medal in the decathlon.

SECTION

ONE

MAKING
YOUR
SELF
BETTER

We define leadership as the ability to make those around you better. This is accessible to everyone – not just the most charismatic or the best player. It's a requirement on our team that every player possess some leadership, and try to make those around him better.

Jack Clark, Rugby Coach, University of California
Winner of 21 National College Rugby Titles

Leadership For Everyone 2.1

Triple-Impact Competitors are leaders who make their teammates better and, as a result, make their teams more successful.

The conventional idea of leadership in this country is a heroic individual who makes things happen pretty much all by himself. This has been called the "genius with a thousand helpers" model. But leadership at its best is a collective effort and truly a team sport. It's no coincidence that great organizations have great leadership teams. Leadership comes in a variety of forms.

Here are leadership essentials for making teammates better.

1) Leadership is a role. It is *not* tied to a title such as coach or captain.

2) Leadership is open to anyone who is emotionally committed to the team's success. It is *not* limited to heroic, charismatic, strong, and/or brilliant individuals who "look like a leader."

3) Leadership is the release of energy. It usually is *not* telling people what to do, especially in a rude or forceful way.

SECTION

TWO

MAKING
YOUR
TEAM
MATES
BETTER

Leadership is a Role

In traditional thinking about leadership, there are official "leaders," and the rest are followers. But in high-performing teams, everyone acts to move the team forward. Teams where followers stand around waiting for the designated leaders to tell them what to do are uninspired and less effective.

Rather than a position or title, think of leadership as a role anyone can play. Actions that move the team ahead are forms of leadership, whether done by the coach, a captain, or a teammate. On great teams, people step up as leaders to act when they see what needs to be done.

For example, you don't have to be a captain to arrive early to practice, set the pace during conditioning drills, or go all-out regardless of the score. You don't have to be a captain to make an underclassman feel like a valued member of the team, invite a shy teammate to join you for lunch, or reach out when a teammate suffers a setback on or off the field. And you don't have to be a captain to praise teammates with gusto or give tough feedback with care. All of this is leadership.

Leadership is also knowing when to follow. There are times when you help your team most by supporting a teammate or coach who takes initiative. You become a "dynamic follower" who knows when to lead, and a leader who knows when to follow.

Leadership is Emotional Commitment

Gene Webb, a mentor of mine at the Stanford Graduate School of Business, was fond of saying, "You can smell emotional commitment a mile away." Someone with an emotional commitment to a cause or to a team draws the commitment of others who also want to be part of accomplishing something important. This is leadership.

SECTION

TWO

MAKING
YOUR
TEAM
MATES
BETTER

Athletes who are emotionally committed don't just go through the motions. They are committed to team success heart and soul, and relentlessly look for ways to help teammates get better so *together* they can accomplish their goals. This means they push hard in practice, despite fatigue or personal distractions. They are vocal and demonstrative in their encouragement. And, when necessary, they willingly sacrifice individual accomplishments to help their team succeed.

This means you don't need to be the smartest person or best athlete on your team to be a leader. An emotional commitment to your team's success qualifies you to play a leadership role.

■ Leadership is the Release of Energy

John W. Gardner, author of *On Leadership*, once told me, "Leadership is the release of energy." Some teams never get untracked, while on other teams things click, everyone pulls together, and the sum is greater than the parts. Teams that perform beyond expectations often have inspired leadership that "releases the energy" of team members.

Some think leadership is yelling and telling people what to do. But people who yell-and-tell rarely gain people's commitment because no one likes being verbally abused or always told what to do. Yell-and-tell shuts people down and kills their leadership potential.

Helping teammates feel part of the team helps release their energy. So does helping younger players see their potential. Tell a younger player you can see her becoming a starter if she keeps working hard, and you may light a fire that will drive her to do exactly that. You can also be the "energy source" for your team – the player who plays with such energy it lifts the whole team. Force a bad pass, get to a ground ball first, make a gritty dig – constant movement and constant hustle is contagious, and the entire team feeds off it.

People contribute energy to a team when they feel excited about working together to achieve a goal. Dictatorial, my-way-or-the-highway behavior usually gets in the way of people committing to a team. So you don't have to yell to lead. Instead, look for positive ways to pull your team together, work hard to build the confidence of your teammates, and show your commitment with constant effort and hustle – all of which release energy.

There are people who bring you down in life. And then there are people who bring you up. You want to be around the ones who fill your tank. We had a lot of them on the team.

Julie Foudy
Co-Captain, U.S. National Team &
FIFA World Cup Champions, 1991 & 1999

2.2 **Filling Emotional Tanks**

People do better when their Emotional Tanks are full. The E-Tank is like the gas tank of a car. If your car's gas tank is empty, you can't drive very far. If you have a full tank, you can go a long way.

Triple-Impact Competitors understand a key way to make team-mates better is to make sure they get their E-Tanks filled on a regular basis.

■ The Portable Home Team Advantage

The home team wins about 60 percent of the time in profes-sional sports. There are several reasons for this, but there is no doubt the emotional support of the fans is a big part of it.

This isn't rocket science. People perform better when they feel better about themselves than when they are down on

SECTION

TWO

MAKING
YOUR
TEAM
MATES
BETTER

themselves. Having people cheer for you makes you feel better and helps you perform better.

When their E-Tanks are full, your teammates are more open to improvement, they are more optimistic, deal better with adversity, have more energy, and respond better to challenges.

If your team members routinely fill each others' tanks, your team can develop a *portable* home team advantage. It's as if you play all your games – home or away – in front of a huge supportive crowd who has your back. And we know that means better results on the scoreboard.

■ Natural Tank Drainers

Humans are natural tank drainers who don't need to be taught how. We are better at draining tanks than filling them, often doing it without even realizing it.

Criticism and sarcasm, which can be very satisfying, are deadly tank drainers. Nonverbal actions like frowning, rolling your eyes, and sighing dramatically also drain E-Tanks. Ignoring someone when he or she speaks? Ditto.

■ Using the Magic Ratio to Fill Teammates' E-Tanks

Triple-Impact Competitors constantly look for opportunities to fill teammates' E-Tanks. And it turns out that it takes a lot of tank filling for people to be able to do their best.

Research indicates optimum performance comes from about five tank-fillers for each criticism. This is called the "Magic Ratio" (5:1) because people improve so much it seems like magic.

Tank fillers can be verbal or nonverbal, extended interactions, or quick hits that take virtually no time. Here are some tools guaranteed to fill the tanks of your teammates, and make your team better, if you employ them.

Tank-Filling Tools	Examples
Names	People love to hear their own name, so use your teammates' names often: "Hey, Gabriel, how's it going?"
Comings & Goings	Greet teammates and say goodbye after practices and games: "Sandra, see you at practice tomorrow!"
Praise	Praise works best when it is truthful and specific: "Enrique, your hustle in the fourth quarter got us all going!"
Express appreciation	Simply saying thanks fills E-Tanks: "Daniella, thanks for showing me how you do that move."
Offering to help	Offering help to a teammate is a potent tank filler: "Need any help getting ready for Friday's game, Ralph?"
Glue actions	Be the person on your team who notices and comments on the unsung things that hold a team together: "Jaya, great pick for Carla on that game-winner. We wouldn't have won without it!"
Check-ins	Look out for teammates who seem down and check in with them: "How you doing, Rashad? You seem a little down today."
Watching out for younger players	If you are an older or more talented player, being friendly to younger or less talented players can make them more confident, more likely to work hard, and a bigger contributor to the team's success.

SECTION

TWO

MAKING
YOUR
TEAM
MATES
BETTER

Tank-Filling Tools	Examples
Asking and listening	Being asked for your ideas and being listened to are big tank fillers: "I'm having trouble getting open on that new route. How do you do it?"
Mistake Ritual (see Chapter 1.4)	A person's tank is lowest after a mistake: "Don't worry, Marjorie, we'll get it back. Just flush it! "
Nonverbal actions	Tank filling doesn't have to be talk. Smiling, clapping, fist bumps, head nods, thumbs up, and eye contact all fill tanks.

Triple-Impact Competitors commit to making their team better by becoming a regular tank-filler. Use Exercise 6 on the following page to create a plan for filling your teammates' E-Tanks this season.

In Chapter 2.2 you learned about the power of filling Emotional Tanks. Here are some ideas for how you can fill your teammates' E-Tanks:

- Give specific, truthful praise during practices and games.
- Invite a teammate you don't know well to join you for lunch.
- Go out of your way to look out for teammates who need extra tank filling.
- Send tank-filling messages via texts or Facebook.
- Rally teammates to go to the junior varsity or freshmen game to root for the younger athletes in your program.
- Identify the kinds of things – music, exercise, games, naps, hanging out, journaling – that fill your own E-Tank and do them regularly.

1. Identify a few teammates who might need tank-filling right now. What specifically can you do to fill their respective E-Tanks?

_____

_____

_____

2. What are you going to do to fill *your* E-Tank during the season?

_____

_____

_____

When things go well, the right people point out the window...they shine a light on other people who contributed to the success and take little credit themselves...when things go awry, they do not blame circumstances or other people...they point in the mirror and say, "I'm responsible."

Jim Collins
Best-selling author and business consultant

Developing Double Vision 2.3

I n 2007, Taylor Rochestie, a junior starter on the Washington State University basketball team that would eventually advance to the Sweet 16 of the NCAA tournament, volunteered to give up his scholarship to allow his coaches to recruit another talented player to make the Cougars a better team the following season.

Rochestie was a good player but not a superstar. It was conceivable that Washington State would recruit someone who would cut into his playing time. Yet he sacrificed scholarship money and risked reduced playing time to help his team get better. Rochestie had what I call "Double Vision."

The Ins and Outs of Double Vision

Triple-Impact Competitors have "Double Vision" – the ability to look both inward and outward for the betterment of the team. The inward view is "Mirror Time," an internal scan of what is going on inside you, including taking a hard look at your feelings and taking personal responsibility for your actions. The outward view is "Window Time," an external scan that involves focusing on what is going on with your team and your teammates so you can help them be successful.

Triple-Impact Competitors ask, "Is it Window Time or Mirror Time?" The answer depends on what your team needs in the moment. Sometimes it's a Mirror, and sometimes a Window. Sometimes it can be both at once. Some examples:

➤ Everyone is down after a tough loss. You played poorly, but others did worse. Go to the Window and blame your hapless teammate, or look in the Mirror and take responsibility for your mistakes? *Mirror:* "We played hard tonight, which is great. I made some bonehead plays, and I'm sorry for putting us in a bad position."

➤ You excelled in a big win. Exult in your good play (Mirror), or give credit to your teammates (Window)? *Window:* "You guys set me up. Sandy, great screen to free me for that last basket. Natasha, fantastic passes inside."

➤ Coach subs you out in an important game. Feel sorry for yourself (Mirror), or keep your head in the game to help your team win (Window)? *Mirror then Window:* "I'm upset I'm not playing, but I'll support Jake so we can win." "Jake, that linebacker keys on where you look when you come to the ball. What if you looked both ways?"

SECTION

TWO

MAKING
YOUR
TEAM
MATES
BETTER   2.3 | Elevating Your Game | 54

Here's a guide to some common situations:

Situation	What time?	Comments
Tough Times (e.g., losing streaks)	Mirror	Lead by example to help the team get through tough times; take responsibility for your mistakes and refuse to blame others.
Success (e.g., winning streaks)	Window	Shine the spotlight on your teammates to give them credit for their contributions rather than trying to get maximum credit for yourself.
Negative Feelings (e.g., jealousy, doubt, fear, anger)	Mirror	Acknowledge negative feelings, but tell yourself: "I'm the kind of person who works to make my team better even when I'm down."
Feedback Opportunities	Window	Share information that could make teammates better, even if it might reduce your playing time.

■ What Can Blur Double Vision

Let's face it — it's not easy to maintain Double Vision. It's complicated because high-performing teams require both cooperation and competition, two things that can conflict.

You cooperate with teammates to try to defeat your opponents, but you compete with them for playing time. Ease up on either and your team doesn't reach its potential. It's hard to win without great teamwork. Fail to compete hard, and you don't develop as a player, nor do you push your teammates to be their best. So being a great teammate requires striking the right balance between cooperation and competition.

Double Vision requires a high level of emotional maturity, something that isn't tied to age as much as understanding the "big picture" about how to make a team function at its best. As a result, Double Vision gets blurred when:

Things go wrong and athletes seek to avoid blame.

> ➤ "It wasn't my fault. That was a terrible call by the official, and Rosalyn blew the pass anyway."

Athletes are passed over and pout.

> ➤ "Why did Coach pull me? I deserve to be out there, not Jackie."

Athletes seek glory for themselves.

> ➤ "I'm going to shoot more so I can be the leading scorer."

■ The Benefit of Selflessness

There is an element of selflessness to being a Triple-Impact Competitor. Sometimes you won't be recognized for your contributions. That's just the way life is. But over time a relentless commitment to making your team better will benefit you. It will make others want you on their team. It will give you opportunities not available to most people.

In the Introduction, I shared the story about how Kurt Warner made Marc Bulger better even though it hurt his chances of regaining his starting position with the Rams. This selfless act paid off when the Arizona Cardinals picked Warner up to mentor their younger quarterback. Instead of being out of the NFL, Warner got the chance to lead the Cardinals to the Super Bowl specifically *because of* his reputation as someone who made his team better, someone with Double Vision.

In the long run, Triple-Impact Competitors win when their team wins because people want to work with people who make them better. Thus, what seems like a sacrifice — putting your team ahead of yourself — turns out not to be a sacrifice at all.

SECTION

TWO
_____

MAKING
YOUR
TEAM
MATES
BETTER

Teams do not succeed by talent alone.

Jeff Janssen
Author, *Championship Team Building*

Team Chemistry and Team Culture 2.4

O ften the difference between successful and unsuccessful teams is an elusive element called "team chemistry," which boils down to how well team members work together and support each other to achieve their goals.

Team chemistry can seem mysterious – a team has it or doesn't, and there isn't much anyone can do about it. But Colleen Hacker, sports psychology consultant to the U.S. National Women's Soccer team for two World Cup championships, says, "Team chemistry is a verb, not a noun." It doesn't just happen, and it requires constant tending, ideally by every member of the team.

Good team chemistry depends on team members believing they will benefit if the team succeeds. When individual players feel valued and recognized for their contributions, they work hard to help the team succeed. However, on many teams, most of the credit goes to star players while important contributions of others are overlooked. This can lead to resentment, factions, and a breakdown of team chemistry.

With a focus on making teammates better, Triple-Impact Competitors are ideally suited to help build good team chemistry.

■ The Qualities of Winning Team Culture

The key to team chemistry is the kind of culture a team has. Culture is simply, "The way we do things here." The habits a team develops are the backbone of its culture and determine whether it develops good team chemistry or not.

In *Championship Team Building,* Jeff Janssen identifies seven qualities of successful teams — elements that breed and result from great team chemistry. Teams with these qualities typically win more, and team members have more fun and memorable experiences. Here are Janssen's qualities, along with specific actions you can take to support each.

Common Goal: Successful teams have goals everyone agrees on. *Action:* Remind teammates about team goals and share your commitment to reaching them. If you are not clear on your team's goals, ask your coach privately about them.

Commitment: Players have a strong work ethic, and tough times are met with determination to work harder. *Action:* Embrace the ELM Tree of Mastery. Focus on effort, learning, and rebounding from mistakes. Be on time and work hard to make yourself and your teammates better.

Complementary Roles: Team members understand and embrace the roles they need to play for team success. *Action:* Become a "superstar at your role." If you are not clear on your role, ask your coach privately about it. Go out of your way to recognize the contributions of everyone, not just the stars.

Communication: Communication is clear, honest, and effective. Players and coaches listen to each other, even in the heat of competition. *Action:* Listening is the communication skill most often lacking on unsuccessful teams, so take time to listen and understand what is important to your teammates.

Constructive Conflict: Team members deal with conflict constructively and openly and don't talk behind each other's backs. Conflict never carries into competition. *Action:* Use your "Double Vision" to balance competing and cooperating with teammates.

Cohesion: Players like being together. They respect each other and help teammates who are struggling. *Action:* People like

SECTION

TWO

MAKING
YOUR
TEAM
MATES
BETTER

being with others who fill their Emotional Tanks, so relentlessly look for oppor-tunities to fill teammates' and coaches' E-Tanks.

Credible Coaching: Caring, competent coaches provide an environment that helps achieve team goals. *Action:* For Triple-Impact Competitors, leadership is for everyone. Step up to lead or follow depending on what the team needs in the moment.

■ Triple-Impact Competitors Make Good Chemists

There's a direct link between Janssen's qualities of successful teams and the mindset of a Triple-Impact Competitor. That's why teams with Triple-Impact Competitors have a leg up in developing great team chemistry. While ordinarily the responsibility for team culture is placed on the coach, on the best teams many members work to create and perpetuate the culture. By focusing on mak-ing teammates better – through acts of leadership, filling E-Tanks, and displaying Double Vision – Triple-Impact Competitors actively work to create and maintain great team chemistry.

Use Exercise 7 on the following page to assess your team's culture and consider how you can contribute to building great team chemistry.

In *Championship Team Building*, Jeff Janssen identifies seven quali-ties that contribute to success. Teams with these qualities not only typically win more, but they have more fun together.

Where is your team on these seven qualities? What can you do this season to promote these qualities on your team?

Team Culture Assessment

1 = Strongly Disagree   2 = Disagree   3 = Agree   4 = Strongly Agree

_____ 1. **Common goal:** Our team has common goals that everyone embraces and works hard to accomplish.

_____ 2. **Commitment:** Team members are committed to our team's success as shown by our work ethic and effort.

_____ 3. **Complementary Roles:** Team members embrace their roles on the team and try to fill them to the best of their ability.

_____ 4. **Communications:** Team members and coaches communi-cate clearly, honestly, and effectively.

_____ 5. **Constructive Conflict:** Team members deal with conflict constructively.

_____ 6. **Cohesion:** Our team is cohesive and likes to be together.

_____ 7. **Credible Coaching:** Our team has credible coaching, and team members demonstrate positive leadership to support coaches' efforts.

What I Can Do to Improve Team Culture

The most important actions I can take to improve team culture are:

1. _____

2. _____

3. _____

4. _____

5. _____

The time is always ripe
to do right.

Martin Luther King, Jr.
Letter From a Birmingham Jail
(April 16, 1963)

3.1 **Preparing For Your "Mallory Moment"**

I t is often when things go wrong that space is created for something remarkable to happen.

Such was the case on Saturday, April 26, 2008, during a Division II softball game between Western Oregon University and Central Washington University.

Although the larger world of sports pays little attention to the Division II college level, the players on the field that day understood that the outcome of the game could help determine which team made it to the NCAA playoffs. Especially for the seniors on these teams, that made this game huge.

In the top of the second inning, with two Western Oregon teammates on base, Sara Tucholsky stroked a ball over the centerfield fence for what seemed like a three-run homer, the first of her career. Because Tucholsky, a senior, was not a starter for her team, this was a big deal for her. She was going out of her college career with a three-run home run in an important game.

In her excitement, Sara missed stepping on first base, realized it, and quickly pivoted to go back to touch first before completing her home run trot. Unfortunately, that pivot landed her in a clump on the ground, with a ligament injury in her right knee.

Now her coaches and teammates were in a tough spot. According to the rules, if anyone on Sara's team touched her, she would be an automatic out, and the third run she had earned with her shot out of the park would be invalidated. Her two teammates had already crossed home plate, so they were not able to aid her.

Sara was in so much pain she wasn't even able to crawl back to first base, let alone complete her trip around the bases. What happened next made this a game that will be remembered as long as people play sports.

After thinking it over, Central Washington first baseman Mallory Holtman approached the umpire: "Would it be okay if we carried her and she touched each bag?" The umpire acknowledged that the rules allowed it. Mallory enlisted her teammate, shortstop Liz Wallace, and they told Sara they would gently carry her back to first base and then to all the other bases. They carefully stooped down so Sara could gingerly touch her left foot to each base.

When Mallory Holtman was asked why she had helped Tucholsky, she said it was the right thing to do because Tucholsky had "earned" a home run by hitting the ball out of the park. It would have been understandable if Holtman had not helped Tucholsky, but the fact that she did elevated the game in dramatic fashion. Her action won an ESPY award from ESPN for "the best moment" in sports that year.

Athletes who compete long enough will find themselves faced with a Mallory Moment, where doing the right thing at the right time elevates the game in an unexpected way.

Your Mallory Moment won't look exactly like Mallory Holtman's moment. It will have its own dimensions, particulars, and look-and-feel. It may not even be much noticed or remembered by onlookers. But count on it — sooner or later, you will be faced with a situation in which you can elevate the game the way Mallory did.

Will you be ready for your Mallory Moment?

> The game is sacred. It's a sacred field you walk on when you go to play. The game is forever; players and coaches are not. When you are out on the field, you must remember your legacy and what you are representing.
>
> **Herm Edwards**
> Former NFL Head Coach

3.2 **The ROOTS of Honoring the Game**

Triple-Impact Competitors make the game better by competing by a code of Honoring the Game. The acronym ROOTS describes behavior that makes the game better—respect for: **R**ules, **O**pponents, **O**fficials, **T**eammates, and **S**elf.

Rules: Triple-Impact Competitors want to win the way the game is supposed to be played. They refuse to bend the rules whether anyone is looking or not. Rules have been developed and carefully modified to make games as fair as possible. Breaking them undercuts fairness.

But rules can't cover every situation. A crafty individual can find a way to circumvent the wording of any rule. Honoring the Game means respecting both the spirit and the letter of the rules.

Opponents: A worthy opponent is a gift. Imagine a tug-of-war with no one at the other end of the rope. Without opponents, competitive sports make no sense. It's also not much fun to beat up on a much weaker opponent (or be dominated by a much stronger one). We are challenged when we have a worthy

SECTION

THREE

MAKING
THE
GAME
BETTER

3.2 | Elevating Your Game | 64

opponent, one who requires our best. The level of play is elevated when evenly matched rivals with mutual respect compete against each other.

We've seen this with great rivalries in every sport. In tennis, for example, Martina Navratilova and Chris Evert pushed each other to greater heights in the 1970s and 1980s. More recently, Roger Federer and Rafael Nadal produced historic matches of incredible tennis that neither would be able to match without the other's challenge.

"Fierce and friendly" says it all. You try as hard as you can to win. If you knock down an opponent going for the ball, you grab the loose ball and try to score. But when the whistle blows, you help your opponent up. Sports gives us the chance to get to know people we compete with, even become friends with them, without ever letting up when the game is on.

Katie Bruzzone, a 2008 finalist for PCA's Triple-Impact Competitor scholarship, saw her high school coach lose control and verbally attack the best player on an opposing team after a game. Katie looked up the opposing player's phone number and called her. "I wanted to personally apologize for the coach's hurtful comments and let her know how much I respect the way she plays the game." Katie was delighted to find that this conversation led to a wonderful long-term friendship with the other player.

Officials: Officials are guides to fairness in the game. Honoring the Game means respecting officials even when they are wrong. There is never an excuse for treating officials with disrespect. Detroit Tigers pitcher Armondo Galarraga impressively demonstrated this on June 3, 2010, when he lost a perfect game on the last out of the game.

Umpire Jim Joyce blew the call at first base that prevented Galarraga from a perfect game. While Tigers Manager Jim Leyland went nuts, Galarraga shrugged off the call and quickly got the next batter out to end the game.

The next day Leyland, who had apologized for his outburst, had Galarraga deliver the line-up to Joyce before the game so he could publicly shake his hand. Galarraga noted about Joyce, who was devastated when he realized his blown call ruined Galarraga's perfect game, "I have a lot of respect for the man. It takes a lot to say you're sorry and to say in interviews he made a mistake." Armando

Galarraga showed what it means to Honor the Game even when an official's mistake hurts — and in his case, hurt a lot.

Teammates: Triple-Impact Competitors never do anything, on or off the field, to embarrass their teammates. They behave in a way so their teammates, school, and family can be proud of them. Because the heat of competition can sometimes bring out the worst in each of us, it helps to develop personal and team routines to reinforce Honoring-the-Game behavior. Exercise 8 describes some routines that other high school and college athletes and teams have used.

Self: Respect for oneself is the foundation of Honoring the Game. Individuals with self-respect would never dishonor the game because they have their own standards that they always want to live up to.

When I'm asked if I expect people to Honor the Game when their opponents don't, I respond, "Of course. That's what having your own standards means." Triple-Impact Competitors maintain their standards even when an opponent lowers his to gain an advantage.

■ Make a Commitment to Honor the Game

The games we love to play deserve to be honored. When athletes like Mallory Holtman Honor the Game (as described in the previous chapter), they make their sport and the world around them better. Use Exercise 8 on the following page to learn how you can develop your own Honor-the-Game routines so you'll be prepared to elevate the game when the right moment presents itself.

SECTION

THREE

MAKING
T H E
GAME
BETTER

As you read in Chapter 3.2, the S in the ROOTS of Honoring the Game stands for respect for one's Self. Triple-Impact Competitors live up to their own standards no matter what the opposition does. But competition is full of challenging situations that arouse our emotions and make this hard to do, such as when:

● An opponent cheap-shots you, talks trash, or cheats

● An official blows a call that hurts you or your team

● You want to win so badly you are tempted to cheat or play dirty

● A teammate or coach says or does something in a game or practice that angers you

Triple-Impact Competitors use Honor-the-Game routines like the ones listed below to control the anxiety, anger, and fear that competition can breed to better handle their emotions.

Appropriate routines can help you perform your best, keep you from doing foolish things that hurt your team (like getting a red card or technical foul, screaming at a teammate, or losing focus by seeking "payback" after an opponent trash talks), and boost your ability to Honor the Game.

Honor-The-Game Routines

1. Develop a self-control routine to use when you feel your emotions building up. Tap your head to remind yourself to "keep a cool head." Take deep breaths, count backwards from 100, or slap your thighs to symbolize moving on. Your routine should help calm you and refocus your attention on the next play.

2. Thank officials before and/or after every game.

3. Shake hands with the opposing coach before and/or after every game.

4. Shake hands with opponents after each game. Look each of them in the eye and say something positive, even after tough defeats.

5. Welcome opponents to your school. This can be done as simply as writing "Welcome, Eagles!" on the visiting locker room whiteboard, or as elaborately as presenting each opponent with a small gift, like a water bottle with "Honor the Game" and your logo on it, before the game. On senior night at one high school, gifts were given to the opposing team's seniors as well. At another high school, the scoreboard was changed to read, "HOME" and "GUESTS" (not "VISITORS"), and players, boosters, and staff were instructed to treat the opposing teams as if they were guests.

6. Before games at many schools, an announcement is made asking coaches, players, parents, and fans to Honor the Game and thanking the officials for their effort. If your school doesn't do this, talk with your coach and athletic director about starting to do it.

List the Honor-the-Game routines you commit to use this year, including those you plan to talk with your coach and teammates about.

1. _____

2. _____

3. _____

It takes a great deal of bravery
to stand up to our enemies, but even
more to stand up to our friends.

Dumbledore
Head of Hogwarts School
Harry Potter and the Sorcerer's
Stone **by J. K. Rawlings**

Finding Your Moral Courage 3.3

In 1947 Jackie Robinson broke the color barrier as the first African-American player in Major League Baseball. Today, with every sport racially integrated, it's hard to imagine how difficult this was. In addition to death threats, Robinson found members of his own team – the Brooklyn Dodgers – didn't want to play with him because of his race.

When the Dodgers played at Crosley Field in Cincinnati in May 1947, Robinson was the target of racist taunts, jeers, and death threats. The Dodgers' captain, Pee Wee Reese, made a point of standing with his arm around Robinson as if to say, "This man is good enough to be on my team, and I stand with him."

Pee Wee's Moral Courage

We often think of physical bravery when we talk about courage, such as a firefighter going into a burning building to rescue a sleeping child. But many of the injustices in the world happen because observers stand idly by because they lack "moral courage." Moral courage is standing up publicly for what you believe is right even when others – including sometimes your friends and teammates – don't.

Jackie Robinson's physical and psychological courage in facing the pressure that dogged his career was enormous. Pee Wee Reese showed moral courage in standing up against the prevailing norm for many in that era which valued black people less than white people.

Reese, the only Southern-raised Dodger who refused to sign a petition against Robinson, went against the grain of his upbringing to stand shoulder-to-shoulder with him. Robinson later credited Reese's support as helping him succeed against all the pressures of being the first African-American player in Major League baseball. This act of moral courage is commemorated in a statue of Reese and Robinson outside the stadium in Coney Island where the minor league Brooklyn Cyclones now play.

■ Running Mindlessly With the Herd

Human beings have a deep need to be part of a group. Mostly this is a good thing, and it has helped humankind in important ways. But there is a downside to it. We can want to be part of a group so much we do things we know are wrong to avoid conflict with others in the group. And sometimes we may not directly participate in wrongdoing but stand idly by while others do bad things.

Because being ostracized from a group is so scary to many people, they are willing to compromise their ethical standards to run mindlessly with the herd. Exhibiting moral courage requires real courage.

■ Standing Up Against Hazing

In recent years terrible high school hazing incidents where older athletes have violently abused younger teammates have made the news. Beyond that, less violent but otherwise degrading forms of hazing regularly occur on many high school sports teams. Each time I hear about a hazing incident, I think of Pee Wee Reese and wonder why no one on these teams tapped their moral courage and stood up for the harassed players, as Reese did for Jackie Robinson. If those teams had any Triple-Impact Competitors on them, they would have defended the abused players.

SECTION
THREE
―――――
MAKING
THE
GAME
BETTER

Sometimes standing up against hazing requires bold action, which can put you crossways with teammates. You may just have to take a vocal and public stand and say, "This is not okay. I'm not going to allow my teammates to be abused." But often a small gesture, or asking a pointed question, can lead people to re-evaluate what they are doing and stop harmful behavior. Still, even that requires being willing to risk being unpopular with your own teammates.

But that is the price of moral courage — and why it is so important in a world where most people can't find theirs.

In our school athletes run the show.

Edgar Gutierrez
Winner, 2008 PCA Triple-Impact
Competitor Scholarship

3.4 Using Your Power to Improve Your School Community

With 12 All-Star appearances, 12 Gold Glove Awards, four National League batting titles, and 3,000 hits, Roberto Clemente was one of the greatest baseball players ever. But what people remember most about Clemente is his work *off* the field.

On New Year's Eve, 1972, Clemente boarded a plane loaded with food, clothing, and medical supplies bound for Nicaragua, which had experienced a devastating earthquake. The loaded-down plane Clemente boarded didn't inspire confidence, but he told his wife, "When your time comes, it comes... And babies are dying. They need these supplies."

Shortly after take-off, the plane crashed in the ocean, killing all five on board. Because of Clemente's courage and sacrifice, high schools, stadiums, bridges, hospitals, and Major League Baseball's humanitarian award bear his name. What does Clemente's story have to do with you?

■ Athletes Have Power

Many high school athletes have status because of what they do on the field. Unfortunately, in many schools a "jock culture" exists in which athletes use their status and influence solely for

SECTION
THREE

MAKING
THE
GAME
BETTER

their own benefit. Whether you realize it or not, you have an incredible opportunity to wield your power on campus in productive ways to make your life and the lives of others around you better.

■ Mentor Younger Athletes

If you reach out to less skilled or younger teammates, or to JV athletes if you are on varsity, you will have a huge impact on how they feel about themselves and on their confidence on the playing field. They may also remember and appreciate your kindness for a lifetime. This might entail simply saying hello to them, showing interest in them on campus or before practice, or "taking them under your wing" to mentor them throughout the season.

■ Include the Excluded

High school is a difficult time for many students who feel alienated from the school community. Students, including athletes, often break into cliques that leave many teens feeling isolated and left out. But it doesn't have to be that way.

Joe Ehrmann, a former NFL Pro Bowl lineman who is now a high school football coach in Baltimore, was the subject of a book by Jeffrey Marx called *Season of Life*. Ehrmann's team has a rule: Nobody eats alone.

If a member of the Gilman Greyhounds football team, often one of the top teams in the country, sees a student eating by himself in the cafeteria, he is required to go and sit with the student or invite him to join the player at his table. Athletes at Gilman make the school better by including those who might otherwise be excluded.

Think about it: when a friend is kind to you, it's nice. When a high-status person you don't know well is kind to you, it can change your entire feeling about school.

■ Help Create an Anti-Bullying Culture

Half of all students report being bullied at some point by the time they leave high school. Ninety percent of gay teens say they were bullied in the previous year. Many say bullying – exerting power through violence, threat of violence, name-calling, insults, gossip, putdowns, trying to damage a person's relationships, or cyberbullying – is the biggest problem in their lives.

The negative impact of bullying – for the bullied, for bullies. and for bystanders – can be long lasting and sometimes tragic. Here are some ideas to help create a bully-free school culture.

● **Set an Example.** Sometimes athletes bully teammates or other kids. So look at your own behavior, and if you are bullying someone, stop. If you have friends who bully, let them know you think bullying is an act of weakness, and that true strength is demonstrated by treating every student in the school with respect.

● **Respond.** If you see someone bullying another student, here are some things you can do that won't escalate the problem.

> ➤ Don't use or threaten the use of force. This often makes things worse. Trust me on this.

> ➤ Assess the situation to see if you can say something without putting yourself or others in danger. You might simply ask a question such as "What's going on?" A question can be disarming and more effective than aggressively confronting a bully.

> ➤ Talk with a trusted school official about the best way to solve this situation.

> ➤ Offer your support to the bullied student and let him know you don't approve of the way he is being treated. This literally can be life saving, as bullied individuals often feel very alone and despairing.

● **Join School-Wide Anti-Bullying Efforts.** Many schools have anti-bullying initiatives, and some state laws require them. If your school has one, get involved with it. If not, talk with school administrators to see if one can be started. Having athletes involved in leadership positions can help such an effort succeed.

SECTION

THREE

MAKING
T H E
GAME
BETTER

3.4 | Elevating Your Game | 74

Bullying is not even good for the bully. Bullying does not help people develop strong relationships or succeed in life. Having a strong anti-bullying culture in your school can help bullies correct their behavior before it ruins their lives.

■ Support Other School Activities

Many school activities do not draw the kind of crowds sporting events draw. Athletes showing up at a play or a concert can mean a lot to the involved students. Having the varsity support the JV team, or the boys' team support the girls' team in the same sport (and vice versa) is also a great program builder.

■ Get Involved in Community Service

A life lived only for oneself is a lonely life. People who help others tend to be happier and more successful than people who don't. High school is a great place to begin a life of serving others, and it can help bring the school community together.

If there is already a school-wide community service initiative, get involved with it. If there isn't such an initiative, consider starting one, and involve non-athletes to help break down divisions within the school.

Fortunately, examples abound of high school community service projects:

> ➤ Organize canned food drives for homeless shelters

> ➤ Collect stuffed animals for a children's hospital

> ➤ Volunteer with Special Olympics or Ronald McDonald House

> ➤ Hold sports clinics for younger athletes

> ➤ Coach or officiate games of younger athletes

> ➤ Visit the elderly in retirement communities

■ Student-Athlete Council

Get involved with your school's student-athlete council to give feedback to the administration and initiate and plan activities. If your school doesn't have one, talk with the athletic director to see about starting one.

■ Athletes and Their Legacies

One of Roberto Clemente's friends remembered him this way. "I think the bottom line for him was trying to show other[s] ... if you dedicate yourself to a cause, you can be a winner."

When you are done with your sport, how will others – teammates, opponents, the excluded classmate, the grade-schooler who showed up to your game, your parents – remember you? Use Exercise 9 on the following page to identify how you will make a difference in your school community.

SECTION
THREE

MAKING
THE
GAME
BETTER

3.4 | Elevating Your Game | 76

Triple-Impact Competitors recognize the power and influence they have as athletes and seek ways to improve their school community. There are a number of ways, large and small, that you can wield your status and influence to make your school a better place. These include:

- Mentoring, coaching, or running clinics for younger athletes.
- Including classmates who otherwise feel excluded. Like Joe Ehrmann says, "No one eats alone."
- Getting involved with anti-bullying activities.
- Supporting other classmates' activities by showing up and cheering them on. This works best at events few attend, like junior varsity games.
- Participating in community service activities as a team or on your own.

1. List what you, your team, or you and a group of teammates can do this season to make a positive contribution to your school community.

_____

_____

_____

2. Create an action plan. As you do, talk to your coach. Bring this topic up at a team meeting. Involve teammates. You'll make a bigger impact with more people involved. Then follow through and make it happen.

_____

_____

_____

> # Life is what happens to you while you're busy making other plans.
>
> **John Lennon**

4.1 **What Do You Do When?**

ometimes the greatest plan in the world isn't enough for handling the challenges of daily life as an athlete, student, teammate, and friend. Here are seven common challenges student-athletes face, with thoughts on ways you can rise to the occasion to meet them.

1 | Way Too Much to Do

Sometimes I just feel overwhelmed. I have practice after school. By the time I get home, it's 6:30. After dinner, homework is stacked up. With other commitments — clubs, volunteering, work (not to mention friends and sleep) — I feel so much pressure. How do I manage this too-full schedule?

SECTION

FOUR

COMMON
CHALLENGES
FOR HIGH
SCHOOL
ATHLETES

My friend, Leo Linbeck III, once told me, "There are no easy jobs with big impact. If you want a stress-free life, recognize you probably won't have much impact."

This is an important insight for Triple-Impact Competitors who want to have a positive impact in the world. Growing involves learning to deal with increased responsibility. As runners or swimmers learn to lower their times by training beyond the point of discomfort, we also learn to handle more as we get outside our comfort zone.

It's also true we may try to do so much we don't do justice to the big things. Too many small things can cloud our vision and overwhelm and discourage us. The key is to decide on your Big Picture and keep focused on it.

Use the "5-Year Rule" to identify your Big Picture. Many of the things we worry about today we won't even remember in five years, but some will be very important. Project five years into the future and look back:

"When I was in high school, I'm glad I _____ ."

Try to limit yourself to no more than 5 things, and don't worry if you don't get them exactly right at first. You can refine this over time.

Keep two lists. A to-do list with the important things you need to do is useful. Just as important is what business expert Jim Collins calls a "Don't-Do List" − the things you won't do to free up time for the important things.

Some things are required − like school. But you don't have to do everything everyone wants. You can decide not to do something. You may have to make some hard decisions and let others know you can't do what they want you to.

A friend's son made the jazz band in his school and decided he couldn't do justice to both lacrosse and jazz band, so he chose to drop lacrosse. He explained his decision to his parents and told his coach he was quitting to focus on music. It may have been hard for him to do this, but he did it. And so can you if you feel too stretched. Look at all your activities, and pick out those that are important to you. Talk with your parents about which ones you want to focus on and which to drop.

Note that some parents live vicariously through the success of their kids. If your parents are like this, you may have to convince them that you will be happier and more successful if you focus on fewer things and do them well. Everyone − including family, coaches, teachers, and friends − is ultimately responsible for his or her own feelings and actions, just as you are responsible for yours. If you are a "people pleaser" who gets uncomfortable when others get upset with you, you may need to learn to live with a little discomfort while you stay true to your own decisions about sports and life.

Schedule time to plan. It may be a cliché, but it is true: "Failing to plan is planning to fail." Set aside 15 minutes each week to get organized (perhaps on Sunday evening). Get Big Picture items on the calendar and allocate enough time to them. Use the Goal-Setting exercise on page 14 for your important goals.

Be better than perfect. Perfectionism is a prescription for failure and unhappiness. If we feel we have to be perfect, we typically won't start work on a project until it is breathing down our neck. Break free of perfectionism and you will have a much happier and more successful life.

As a teenager I worked in the North Dakota sugar beet fields. One day the foreman told me I was doing "too good" a job. He noticed I worked slower than others because I was determined to get every last weed. He explained that beets could grow fine with a few weeds here and there. I was trying to be perfect with something that didn't require perfection.

As my friend Greg Tehven told me, "Perfect is good. Done is better." Many things don't need to be perfect — they just need to get done. If you try to be perfect where you don't have to, you steal time from things that do need to be done well, such as college application essays. Identify things that just need to be done and get them out of the way.

Get a head start. An early start on a big project is liberating, so don't wait until crunch time. Log time early on what Anne LaMott in *Bird by Bird* calls "crummy first drafts." Completing a draft, even a bad one, plants a stake in the ground. Crummy first drafts lead to not-so-bad second drafts, good third drafts, and so on. An early start creates momentum that may be the difference between a so-so effort and a really good one.

Eat, sleep, appreciate. Food and sleep are fuel for humans. Eat healthy — munch on apples or carrots rather than junk food. See Exercise 3 on page 21 for more on eating right.

Fatigue makes everything harder, so get enough sleep — research shows teens need 9.25 hours a night. Sneak in a nap when you can.

Life goes by quickly so make time to appreciate the daily joys of life. Make a date with yourself to do something that invigorates you — including unstructured downtime — and put it on the calendar. Being on the calendar makes it seem important, and this is. When doing something to invigorate yourself, don't let your mind wander to all the things you have to do. They'll still be there when you return to them with fresh energy.

2 | Teammates Don't Care

I want to help my team do well, but some of my teammates don't seem to care as much as I do. What can I do about unmotivated teammates?

You will work with people with differing levels of commitment throughout your life. It is actually rare to be part of a unified group of people who are all equally committed to the same goal. Here are some thoughts on dealing with this situation.

Reframe. Reframe this as an opportunity to work on your leadership skills and help your teammates improve. (See page 36 for more on reframing.) NBA star Shane Battier is known for making every team he is on better. Take this season as a personal challenge to work on being the kind of person who makes every team you are on better. And stay positive and keep working hard — you'll stand out if you do, especially if others on the team do not.

Empathize to understand. Empathy is putting yourself in another's situation so you can understand how that person sees things. Understand that your teammates may have a lot going on in their lives, such as family issues, conflicts with friends, money or health problems, or stress around schoolwork. Empathizing with teammates will increase your ability to influence them. Being angry because of their lack of commitment will make it harder for them to respond favorably to your leadership.

Share your emotional commitment. Your emotional commitment to your team can draw the commitment of your teammates. Lead by example with your effort and enthusiasm, as well as your words (see next point).

Reward what you want to see. People do what gets rewarded. And being noticed is rewarding. So comment favorably whenever you see someone trying. Most people get so little reinforcement for doing something well that some E-Tank-filling comments from you can go a long way. You can be a enthusiastic cheerleader or it can be a simple, "Hey, way to push hard!"

Recognize your limits. Ultimately you can't control anyone's behavior. By staying positive and developing the habits of working hard and filling E-Tanks, you are building a foundation for success in life regardless of how this season turns out.

3 | Wanting to Play College Sports

I'd like to play my sport in college, but I also want to go to a good school that suits me. How can I have a great college experience that includes athletics?

Playing college sports can be a fantastic experience. It is also frustrating and disappointing for many athletes. Here are ideas about how to approach this challenge.

Avoid "anchoring." Choosing a college is multi-faceted, so try not to anchor on a single aspect. Anchoring is overvaluing one factor and devaluing all other aspects in a decision.

As a kid, my family looked at an apartment with a dartboard on the door that fascinated me. I wanted to live in that apartment because I was anchored on the dartboard. This is obviously silly, but even many grown people anchor on one appealing but relatively unimportant aspect of a decision as I immaturely did then. When people anchor on a single factor, they tend not to make good decisions.

Consider all aspects of your collegiate experience. Here are three crucial elements of a great college experience for a student-athlete.

■ **The Athlete Experience.** What would it be like to play for these coaches? Would you still want to be at this school if the head coach leaves before you graduate? Do you like the players? You're going to spend a lot of time with your teammates, so it helps a lot if you like each other. What if you don't fulfill your expectations? What if you get injured or spend four years on the bench? Will you still feel good about attending this school?

College athletics is a big commitment. Athletes sometimes feel like they have a full-time job on top of their coursework. Are you ready to take on the workload that college sports require, or might you be happier as a club sport athlete?

■ **The Student Experience.** Are faculty members accessible to students? Are classes mostly huge lectures or are they small enough to get to know your professors? If you know what you want to study, is this school strong in that area? If you're not sure, does this school have a range of studies that might appeal to you?

Are the students people you'd like to spend time with? Do they have different backgrounds and experiences that you can learn from, or are they all pretty similar to you? Are this school's activities, speakers, programs, and cultural activities interesting to you? A school with lots of different things going on is great for widening your horizons.

■ **The Alumni Experience.** When you graduate from a college, you become a lifetime member of its alumni community. It may not be fair, but people may make assumptions about you for the rest of your life by where you went to college. Being part of an alumni community that shares your interests is helpful. Which college will help you develop a rewarding life after graduation? Which college will help you with finding a job in a career that is meaningful to you? If you are interested in wildlife management but most of a school's alumni are in engineering, for example, they may not be much help.

List your priorities for college and use them in your decision making. Rate each school with a 1 to 10 score for athletics, academics, and alumni. If geography, social life, cost, proximity to relatives, or another aspect of college is important, rate it also. Use your ratings to help you in your decision-making. As you learn more about each college on your list, you can change your ratings to reflect new information.

Expand before you narrow. There are thousands of colleges in the United States and likely dozens that would be a good fit for you. There will come a time to narrow your focus to a few schools. But consider a range of schools before you settle on the smaller number that you want to really concentrate on.

Ask around. Ask adults you respect – family and friends, coaches, college athletes – about their college experience. In grade school I wanted to go to the U. S. Naval Academy. My mom asked a relative of ours to tell me about his experience at Annapolis and in the Navy. After talking with him, I realized that the U.S. Naval Academy was not the best fit for me. I eventually narrowed my choice down to two schools and had a great experience at Macalester College in Minnesota, partly because I knew a lot about what I would experience there.

Sample the goods. When you have narrowed your decision, go and visit the finalists. Sit in on classes, attend team practices, stay in the dorm if possible. Employees of the school (coaches, professors, admissions officers) have a vested interest in your liking the school. Students may be more objective, so ask them. Most students, if approached by a prospective student, are happy to share their experience.

Set yourself up for success. Once you know where you want to go, here's how to make it more likely you can do so.

- **Keep your grades up.** The better your grades, the more options you have. Coaches don't want to waste a scholarship or their time and effort on a player who cannot make it in the classroom. If you can't balance athletics and academics in high school, it's not going to get easier in college. Good grades create greater interest in you among college coaches (and college admissions offices).

- **Make sure you are NCAA eligible.** The NCAA has rules for high school athletes, including courses you must take in high school to be able to play in college. Become familiar with NCAA clearinghouse rules at www.ncaa.org. See a school counselor to make sure you are taking the classes needed.

- **Make college coaches aware of you.** Promote yourself. Call and e-mail the coaches of the programs you are interested in. After talking with them, if there is mutual interest, put together a recruiting package including a photo, resume, and highlight DVD. Mail it to the coach with a personalized cover letter.

  Learn how to get noticed in your sport. In track or swimming, great times speak loudest. Volleyball players get noticed by playing on the right club teams and going to the right tournaments. College baseball recruiters go to "showcases" where they watch prospective players. In tennis, your USTA ranking is key. Talk to college athletes in your sport to find out how they got noticed.

- **Be open to different levels.** Athletes can get star-struck about playing at a Division I school when the best combination of academics and sports may be a Division II or III school (which only offers academic or need-based scholarships). Many athletes transfer or quit because they chose a level above where they best fit.

- **Stay focused on your priorities.** Keep your priority rankings in mind. If you attract a lot of attention, you may get a pile of letters and calls. If a school doesn't fit your priorities, remove it from your list. When coaches from those schools contact you, do them a favor. Let them know you are not considering them so they can turn their attention to other recruits.

Keep an open mind. As you go through this process to choose a college, try to remain open until you are ready to make your decision. You may find you want a very different college experience than you thought you did at the beginning of this process. And, remember, despite how much your parents, coach, or friends may want you to go to a particular college, you are the one who will live with this decision the rest of your life. It is your decision, not theirs.

4 | Ouch! Dealing with Injuries

I've been injured pretty badly. My team needs me, and I want to get back to playing as soon as possible. What should I do?

Getting injured and riding the pine can be one of the most frustrating experiences for any athlete. It can also be a time of growth. How can you make the most of it?

Get great advice for how to get back to your sport. Sports trainers, your doctor, and physical therapists are your best source of rehabilitation information.

Approach your rehabilitation like you do practices and games. Work hard in rehab, just like you do in practice. Listen to your rehab "coaches" (the medical experts). Chart your progress, no matter how small. Celebrate "wins" along the way. Given the right effort, the result − your good health − is likely to take care of itself.

Recognize that injuries can have an upside. When I was sidelined in high school with a broken rib on my right side, I spent hours dribbling and shooting a basketball with my left hand. I also learned to open my locker and brush my teeth left-handed. Use injury time to work on areas that you can improve on without compromising your recovery.

Resist the pressure to come back too soon. People may encourage you to rejoin the team before you are fully healed. Resist this pressure. Listen to your doctor or trainer and return only when you are fully healed. Your lifelong health may be at stake, and risking it to come back too soon will be seen as crazy later in life.

Ask your coach how you can help the team. You might analyze videotape of future opponents, mentor younger players, or chart statistics during games. You might serve as team journalist writing stories about the team for the school paper or the team's web site. And you can always fill your teammates' E-Tanks during practices and games.

5 | Coach Problems

I can't go into all of the reasons why, but I don't get along with my coach. How can I play for someone I have problems with?

When athletes click with a coach, it is terrific. But many athletes and coaches don't. Nonetheless, the smart ones find ways to work together for the betterment of the team. Here's how you can do this.

Recognize that coaching is hard. Some coaches make coaching seem effortless, but it isn't. Coaching is difficult, especially for new coaches and recent head coaches. Knowing this may make it easier for you to feel empathy for your coach.

Don't let this ruin your sports experience. You will have talented and untalented supervisors your whole life. Don't let the quality of your experience depend on the quality of your supervisor. Make a commitment to yourself to stay positive and give your best effort to make this season the best it can be.

Focus your energy. Don't waste your limited energy talking trash about your coach with your teammates. This can create a downward spiral that may only make things worse as negativity feeds hungrily on negativity. Focus on things you can control to make yourself and your team better. When players give their best effort and stay positive, a good season is more likely than if they waste energy and time bad-mouthing their coach, as satisfying as that may feel.

Don't talk "out of school." I am unimpressed when people complain to me about their boss or the organization they work for. Although it may be tempting to complain about your coach with people outside the team, avoid it whenever possible. Ultimately people will respect you for keeping your team's dirty laundry private (with one exception – see the last point below).

Consider talking with the coach. Many, but not all, coaches are open to feedback, especially when offered in a helpful, non-confrontational manner. If you think there are changes your coach could make to improve the situation, consider talking with him. Make an appointment to speak with your coach in private. Script your key points, and try them out on a trusted friend or adult. Approach the coach with respect, stay calm, and tell him your concerns.

Take action when your coach is abusive. When a coach is verbally or physically abusive, you need to speak with the athletic director or principal. Talk with your parents so they are not surprised. Think through what you want to say, and write it down. Ask the athletic director or principal for his advice and what he is going to do. Let him investigate and take action while you work on staying positive and working hard.

6 | Cliques and Conflict

My team is divided into cliques who only hang out with each other. Now two groups are fighting. We are supposed to be a team! What can I do about this?

Groups can be scary to a lone individual, so people often try to make friendships with others to protect themselves within a larger group. High school is an especially hard time for many teens, so it's not surprising that they form friendly alliances with people who will accept and appreciate them. But groups degrade to become cliques when they shut people out and become instruments of criticism and cruelty. When cliques infect a team, they can break down team unity and lead to division and conflict. So, what can you do about it?

Proactively reach out to those who are not part of your group. Extend yourself beyond your group of friends. Start conversations with individual teammates you don't know well. Often, you can get to know someone best in a one-on-one situation. Ask different teammates to do something together – going to a movie or a restaurant or your home. Being on a team is great for getting to know people you'd never know otherwise. Don't miss a chance to make new friends and unite your team to prevent cliques from forming.

If you are excluded from a clique, understand it is not about you. People who put others down are mostly insecure about themselves. Don't think less of yourself because you are excluded.

Bring conflict or problems out into the open. When teams are divided, talking things through in the open can help. If you have an issue with another athlete, address it head on, face to face, usually in private. If a coach can help with this, ask him. But don't ignore problems or make things worse by talking down your teammates behind their backs.

Look for opportunities. Sometimes things happen that give you the chance to reach out to a teammate you don't know well, such as filling her E-Tank. If you remain open and look for opportunities to bring the team together, you are likely to find them. Pick your spots and stay positive.

7 | Tempted to Cheat

I work out year-round and lift weights regularly, but I can't keep up with a couple of my teammates who have added a lot of muscle in a very short time. I suspect they are using steroids. Why shouldn't I use them since I am at a competitive disadvantage without them?

Performance-enhancing drugs are cheating, and Triple-Impact Competitors don't cheat. They live up to their own standards (the S in ROOTS stands for Self) even when others don't. There will always be cheaters in every aspect of life. Sometimes they get caught; sometimes they get away with it, at least for a while.

But cheaters always pay a price. For example, steroids have severe negative health impacts including hair loss, shrinking testicles, angry mood swings, sleep problems, nausea and vomiting, high blood pressure, greater chance of muscle injuries, aching joints, jaundice, shortening of adult height, and acne.

But the main thing to remember is that as important as it is to do well in your sport, as a Triple-Impact Competitor, cheating is not part of who you are.

Workshop Evaluation

Date: _____

PCA Presenter: _____

Your organization or school: _____

Gender: ☐ Male ☐ Female   Your Age: _____

Ethnicity: ☐ White ☐ African-American
(check all
that apply) ☐ Latino ☐ Asian-American ☐ Other: _____

Sports you are representing today: _____

Age group you play/coach/parent: _____

To help us do a better job, we need your feedback. Thank you very much!

		POOR	AVERAGE		EXCELLENT	
1.	Overall workshop	1	2	3	4	5
2.	Presenter's effectiveness	1	2	3	4	5
3.	Content of the workshop	1	2	3	4	5
4.	Length of the workshop	☐ Too Short	☐ Just Right		☐ Too Long	

		NOT AT ALL			VERY WELL	
5.	Did your presenter clearly explain PCA's concepts and tools?	1	2	3	4	5
6.	Did your presenter keep you engaged during the workshop?	1	2	3	4	5
7.	Did your presenter effectively respond to participant questions and concerns?	1	2	3	4	5

		DISAGREE			AGREE	
8.	I intend to use workshop ideas this year	1	2	3	4	5
9.	I would recommend others attend this workshop	1	2	3	4	5

10. The best part of this workshop was: _____

_____

11. A way to improve this workshop is: _____

_____

Become a PCA Member Today!

For as little as $25 per year, you can help PCA make a difference in the lives of hundreds of thousands of athletes every year!

As a member, you will be invited to hear podcasts and webinar discussions featuring top athletes and coaches like Summer Sanders, Doc Rivers, and Steve Young. You'll also get a Triple-Impact Competitor Bag Tag to give to a student-athlete!

Yes, I want to make a difference in youth sports by donating:

☐ $25

☐ Other Amount _____

Your Name _____

Street Address _____

City, State, Zip _____

Phone_____

Email _____

☐ Please make my gift anonymous

☐ I/We work for a matching gift company

To sign up online, visit **http://donate.positivecoach.org/Membership**

Or mail this form to:

Positive Coaching Alliance
Attn: Membership
1001 N. Rengstorff Ave., Suite 100
Mountain View, CA 94043